WITHDRAWN

illegitimate

How a Loving God
Rescued a Son of Polygamy

Brian Mackert

David C Cook
transforming lives together

ILLEGITIMATE
Published by David C. Cook
4050 Lee Vance View
Colorado Springs, CO 80918 U.S.A.

David C. Cook Distribution Canada
55 Woodslee Avenue, Paris, Ontario, Canada N3L 3E5

David C. Cook U.K., Kingsway Communications
Eastbourne, East Sussex BN23 6NT, England

David C. Cook and the graphic circle C logo
are registered trademarks of Cook Communications Ministries.

The Web site addresses recommended throughout this book are offered as a
resource to you. These Web sites are not intended in any way to be or imply an
endorsement on the part of David C. Cook, nor do we vouch for their content.

All Scripture quotations are taken from the *Holy Bible, New International
Version®. NIV®.* Copyright © 1973, 1978, 1984 International Bible
Society. Used by permission of Zondervan. All rights reserved.

LCCN 2008933684
ISBN 978-1-4347-6691-5

© 2008 Brian Mackert
Published in association with the literary agency of WordServe Literary
Group, Ltd., 10152 S. Knoll Circle, Highlands Ranch, CO 80130

The Team: Don Pape, Susan Tjaden, Amy Kiechlin, Jack Campbell, and Karen Athen
Cover Design: David Uttley, The DesignWorks Group
Cover Photo: Johnny Franz/Johner Images/Getty Images (boy)
All photos except for the image of the boy on the front cover and the
author photo on the flap are owned and copyrighted by the author.

Printed in the United States of America
First Edition 2008

1 2 3 4 5 6 7 8 9 10

080108

For my Lord and Savior, Jesus Christ — you united me to
the Father of the fatherless.

For my son, Sterling — you're still the keeper of my heart.
I have loved you from the moment I first laid eyes on you, and
that love will never die.

Contents

Acknowledgments

There are people whose contributions to this book and my life cannot go unmentioned.

Dana—you set me free so I could write this book.

Rachel—you believed in me and in this book. Without your encouragement, I would still be working on it. Fifteen minutes a day accomplishes a lot.

Marcus—you offered faithful friendship, mentoring, and encouragement. You planted the seeds about how important it was to tell this story.

My brother Howard—you were the first light of the gospel my eyes ever saw.

My sister Mary—you have always prayed for me, had strong words of truth for me, and have never given up on me.

My many brothers—you have played a major role in my development as a man. You stepped into the void our father left. You weren't always perfect, but you were there.

My sisters who came forward about the abuse in our family—you are among the bravest people I've ever met.

My mom—you got out when you did and took me with you. Although you still hold to the principle of plural marriage, you have sacrificed yourself to help your children heal. You made yourself available to those who have issues and need healing. You weren't always there for us growing up, but you have been there for us as adults as we try to reconcile the past. Your efforts have not gone unnoticed. I, for one, am grateful for the things you've done and love you dearly.

A Word from the Publisher

Illegitimate.

That's a word with instant negative connotations—parents *not* married, *not* lawful, *not* a rightful claim, *not* authorized, *not* the regular way things are done.

Every one of these inferences is true of Brian Mackert's life. His mother and father were not legally married to each other. His family's polygamous lifestyle had no lawful standing. His religious surroundings were a long way outside the norm in American culture. He grew up with an underlying inbred fear of *not* being worthy of God's love and approval. Or anyone's.

This was more than just a dysfunctional family, however. It was more than parents who didn't quite get their act together. Brian's family belonged to the Fundamentalist Church of Jesus Christ of Latter Day Saints—the FLDS that has come into the recent media not only because of a lifestyle that piques curiosity, but also because of the powerful control of its leader, Warren Jeffs, before his imprisonment.

People on the outside scratch their heads. Why are members of the FLDS so adamant about polygamy? Why would people in their right minds let someone like Warren Jeffs control their lives? Why isn't it obvious to "these people" that marrying teen girls to much older men is, well, not appropriate.

All of us look at the FLDS and events of recent years through our own lenses, through the grid of what our own culture and experiences teach us to look for. But what if your culture and experience yield a very different grid? International travelers run into culture shock all the time. Even different regions within one country have cultural distinctives. Traditions and unwritten protocol don't always make sense—they just *are*. Children growing up absorb the culture in a way that no outsider ever will.

Our Western mind-set craves logic and explanation, but those are not always easy to come by. The culture of the FLDS cannot be reduced to a list of bullet points that explains everything to complete satisfaction. However, Brian Mackert grew up in the culture of the FLDS, so his story helps to unravel some tangled threads for the rest of us. For those unfamiliar with Mormon doctrine, particularly fundamentalist interpretations, Brian identifies key theological premises undergirding the FLDS way of life. He looks at the FLDS culture from the inside, not the outside. And through his eyes, we see a grid where polygamy and arranged marriages make sense; we see the FLDS theological truths that demand the lifestyle most of us can't understand—including submission to a man like Warren Jeffs.

As we follow key events in the history of the FLDS, we see where it began to unravel—and how, as threads came loose, particular individuals fought to hold the fabric together by advocating the "one-man doctrine," and in so doing eventually made it possible for Warren Jeffs to exercise absolute control in the lives of his followers. Key points in Brian Mackert's life paralleled key turning points in the FLDS. Brian's own family came unraveled in the midst of the unrest within the FLDS, and Brian began to see that not every untangled thread belongs in the picture.

The Mackert boys and the Jeffs boys played football together. Their families worshipped together on Sundays. Brian Mackert's father and

Warren Jeffs's father both ran prominent schools for the children of the FLDS. Yet Brian Mackert and Warren Jeffs grew up to be two very different men. What made the difference?

Illegitimate: How a Loving God Rescued a Son of Polygamy recounts Brian's journey from a life of hierarchy and unworthiness to a secure place in the family of God. It brings hope to those trapped in deccit and unforgiveness as the light of the gospel shines into dark lives.

Prologue

It was getting late in the afternoon, and I was anxious for the day to end so I could head home from what had been another typical day working as a fiber-optics engineer. I climbed into my Jeep, pulled out of the business complex where I worked, and headed toward my apartment. I was looking forward to a tall glass of iced tea and watching the sunset from my porch swing.

My cell phone jangled. "Hello?"

"Brian, have you seen the news yet?" I immediately recognized the voice as my older sister Rena's.

"No, what's happened?" I asked.

"Go turn on the TV," she insisted. "They've raided the FLDS compound in Eldorado, Texas."

"What! You're kidding me, right?"

"No, it's real! They've finally done it!" Triumph pulsated through Rena's voice.

"I'm on my way home right now," I said. "I'll have to check it out! What started it? What charges are they using to go into the compound?"

"There were several phone calls from a girl claiming to be sixteen and being abused," she informed me.

I promised to call her back once I reached my apartment and had turned on the news. Rena and I had performed this ritual on numerous other occasions in the past as news broke about events surrounding the FLDS Church, its members, and especially its spiritual leader and

Prophet, Warren Jeffs. When a warrant was issued for the arrest of Warren Jeffs on charges of rape by accomplice, Rena called me. When Warren Jeffs made the FBI's Ten Most Wanted list and was featured on the TV crime program *America's Most Wanted*, again Rena called me. When Jeffs was arrested, put on trial, and convicted on two counts of rape by accomplice, Rena called me. With each call we would bemoan events revealed in the media, our own struggles to break free from this cult, and the inability of law enforcement to prosecute the laws against polygamy in their state.

When I turned on the TV and reached for the phone, I paused and watched in amazement as children were put on buses and taken into custody as wards of the state of Texas. A wave of fear from the past surged through me, as I remembered how we lived our childhood in constant fear of a raid on our community—like the one in 1953 in Short Creek, Arizona, when my mother was pregnant with Rena. Because of that raid, we were taught to lie to conceal our family's relationships with each other in order to protect our father's identity as a polygamist. I remembered every time I slipped up and almost let the cat out of the bag, the fear of being the one responsible for launching another raid, the terror of police officers storming our home and snatching us away from our parents, from our home, from each other, and being forced to face the unknown future alone in a world that was completely foreign to us. For us nothing was more frightening than being forced into a world that we were taught hated us and wanted to destroy us because we were God's chosen people.

I nearly jumped out of my skin when my cell phone began to vibrate in my hand, even before swelling to a real ring. It was Rena again, wanting to know if I was home yet. From our separate homes, we watched the news together and commented on details as they unfolded, but our jaws dropped in amazement as the size and scope of this event seemed to increase exponentially. First it was only fifty-three children taken, and then it was over one hundred, then two hundred, then four hundred. Where and when would it end? Suddenly this had become the largest single raid of a polygamist community in history, almost doubling the size of the raid in 1953.

My sisters Rena and Laura had been long-time advocates and activists in trying to get the government to take seriously the allegations of abuse going on within the FLDS Church. For fifteen years they had been speaking out in the media and trying to bring attention to the problems that the government habitually ignored. In that moment I had never been more proud of the state of Texas. Finally someone was willing to do the right thing, to put their necks on the line and fight for the victims of the FLDS Church's rampant abuse of young girls.

"Rena, today all the claims made by you, Laura, and Mary in the media have been validated," I said. Our sister Mary is a Baptist missionary to the polygamists, trying to help those who want out. She, too, has been in the media addressing the abusive nature of polygamist communities, although she isn't an activist.

Over the next few days, reports began to flood the news about girls as young as thirteen or fourteen being pregnant. As some of my other siblings also followed the story, we all searched the faces on TV to see if we could find anyone we recognized, perhaps even a family member, but editors had blurred out all of the faces. We jumped on the Internet and began searching the photos offered there. We did find one almost immediately—showing my sisters Carole and Andrea. Since neither had children, they weren't personally affected by the raid, but their poignant expressions carried the pain they felt about what was happening to their community.

My heart began to ache. I knew far too well the pain those women and children would have ahead of them if they wanted out of this lifestyle.

Theirs would be a long road to recovery, and many might not ever fully heal. Even now news out of the FLDS communities still grips me and my siblings who have left that life. Even after being apart from the FLDS for all these years, the pull of the doctrine and culture on the psyche is powerful. *Are we ever free from the past?* I wondered. *Or is it forever a part of us that we cannot completely bury?*

I thought that my own issues had been dealt with and neatly tucked away, compartmentalized, and filed in alphabetical order. But as I watched the news that night, the past imploded on me in a flood of memories I had to recover from, and I wept at the thought of facing those demons again. I wept at the thought of how these girls would have to face their issues, and I couldn't help but pray that they would take advantage of this opportunity to make their escape too.

My story flashed back to nearly eighteen years earlier in a psychiatrist's office in San Diego, California.

1

Tell Me about Yourself

*My son John: You have asked me concerning the New
and Everlasting Covenant and how far it is binding
upon my people. Thus saith the Lord. All commandments
that I give must be obeyed by those calling themselves
by my name unless they are revoked by me or by
my authority and how can I revoke an everlasting
covenant ... I have not revoked this law nor will I for
it is everlasting and those who will enter into my glory
must obey the conditions thereof, even so Amen.*

*—1886 Revelation to John Taylor, president of the
LDS Church, in hiding from federal marshals*

I wanted to kill my father.

Not metaphorically. Literally. A lifetime of deceit, neglect, and intimidation by this vile man was pushing me toward an explosion I couldn't stop on my own. Reluctantly I agreed to get help to deal with my homicidal thoughts.

The psychiatric ward of the Balboa Naval Hospital in San Diego was the last place I wanted to be, which made this man in front of me the last person I wanted to talk to. I don't know what I expected—or why. After all, I had no prior experience with mental-health professionals. I tried not to roll my eyes visibly as I sized up the man who unfolded from behind the desk to greet me. He looked completely ordinary, with thick black hair buzzed short on the sides, but on top as long as navy regulations would permit. A long hooked nose reminded me vaguely of a vulture's beak. Funny the things you notice.

After shaking the doctor's hand, I lowered myself into the chair opposite his and put on my best imitation of looking relaxed—which I definitely was not. We hadn't even started talking yet, and already I was wrung dry. Just getting through the massive mound of paperwork and psychological evaluations that had thrust me toward this moment had sapped me.

I had every expectation of being overmedicated and institutionalized before day's end. Like so much of my life, I figured I wouldn't have a say. *Do they have a straightjacket in my size,* I found myself wondering, *or are they one-size-fits-all?*

He began by verifying information from my file to ensure proper documentation of my case: name, rank, social security number, unit, and so on. It didn't take long to convince me that I would be just a number to him—a properly documented case number, but a number nonetheless. But so what? Being a number was the story of my life.

By the time we finished the paperwork, our time was almost up, and I had reached the conclusion that this was all a waste of time anyway. Maybe I wouldn't come back. Maybe this was the end. Maybe I would just go kill my father and be done with it.

"Are you comfortable?" he then asked.

Here we go, I thought. *The quack in the sailor suit wants to psycho-analyze me now.*

I assured him I was fine, though clearly I was not. Does someone who is fine want to kill his father?

"It says here you've come to us seeking help dealing with your homicidal thoughts and feelings toward your father."

I nodded, about all I could manage at the moment.

"We don't have time to get into much today, but do you mind if I ask a few simple questions?"

"Why not?" I replied, relieved that this would all be over soon.

"Are you in danger of hurting yourself or anyone else?" he asked. "Have you had any thoughts of suicide?"

"No," I answered, "but the longer I'm here the more appealing the prospect becomes."

His laugh acknowledged my attempt to inject humor into a nerve-racking situation, but the way he kept one eye on me said he wasn't sure if it was a joke or a cry for help.

"Well, if you're sure you're all right," he finally said, "help me get to know you better. Tell me about yourself." He sat with his pen poised over a notepad.

You would have thought he had asked me to define the meaning of life in ten words or less, or to explain the origins of life, or to answer the conundrum of whether a falling tree makes a sound if no one is there to hear it. I could think of a hundred questions that would have been easier to answer than to tell this man about myself. Where would I begin? How would I describe myself to a stranger?

It was a trick, I decided, one of those things psychiatrists do to make you stumble so all your insides dump out where they can pick through them and decipher the significance of stuff no one else recognizes. The clock's ticking was suddenly louder, the room's temperature hotter, my throat tighter, the air thicker. I couldn't breathe. Yet he just sat there with his pen ready, as if he could put my life on a yellow notepad, but I knew I couldn't begin to answer the question in the time we had left in the session.

The silence became excruciating. I started picking aircraft grease out from under my fingernails to avoid lifting my eyes to meet his gaze. Surely he would realize this was going nowhere and give up. But apparently the protracted silence was only uncomfortable for me, not for him. He just waited, watching me, his eyes steadfast in their hunt for clues. My eyes darted to the window, seeking escape from my discomfort, but I remembered we were on the fifth floor. My only escape was the door, and I was sure a squad of orderlies would be at his beck and call to prevent an early end to our session. Still, I wanted to bolt and run.

Yet strangely, I also wanted to talk. I needed to talk. I had willingly agreed to this appointment in the first place—sort of. I saw it as a last resort. But I'd had this tell-me-about-yourself conversation before, with people I'd met and tried to befriend, and I knew the bewilderment that would cross his face as soon as I began to talk about my family. Few people in the general American population had ever met a freak like me. The questions would erupt, and I would have to tell him my whole convoluted story.

By the time I arrived in my parents' home on a cold winter's day, January 9, 1967, I was the twenty-eighth child of a family living in fear that any day the police would come, take our father away, and place us all in foster homes.

Sounds like a movie plot line. But it wasn't.

This reality devoured an enormous percentage of my family's emotional energy. We belonged to the Fundamentalist Church of Jesus Christ of Latter Day Saints, or the FLDS Church. My father eventually had four wives and thirty-one children. Polygamy, though, was not among the religious freedoms we were permitted to practice openly. The roots of our faith were firmly planted in the history of the Church of Jesus Christ of Latter-day Saints (LDS Church), but over the course of a hundred years, we had become an embarrassment to the LDS Church, which had officially abandoned polygamy as long ago as 1890. We broke away when they began excommunicating polygamists. The practice of polygamy, or plural marriage, continued within the LDS Church in secret until around the 1930s, when they began cracking down on it. The fundamentalists, though, didn't give up easily.

JOSEPH SMITH founded the Church of Jesus Christ of Latter-day Saints because of a vision he claimed to have received from an angel in 1827. This angel, Moroni, told him of a hidden record written on golden plates bound together in a book prepared for the purpose of restoring the original gospel of Jesus to its pure form, and reestablishing Christ's true Church. The current gospel was believed to be full of corruption, and the priesthood authority essential to the Church was taken away; there was no longer a single man on earth who held the authority to act in God's name. Moroni led Smith to a hillside near Palmyra, New York, where the angel had hidden these plates of gold and a pair of "seer stones" to help him translate the *Book of Mormon* from this ancient book written in "Reformed Egyptian." Smith founded the church in 1830 and began secretly teaching polygamy only one year later, then started secretly practicing it just three years after the church's founding. As early as July 17, 1831, Smith said that God revealed to him that only a man with at least three wives could enter heaven. This became one of the earliest clandestine teachings and practices of the new church. Our polygamous family stood in a long tradition of religious conviction that set us apart from the outside world.

AGAINST A history of hostility toward polygamists, the fear of my father's arrest and our subsequent placement into the foster-care system because of our religious beliefs was not far-fetched in the least. In July 1953, 120 Arizona state police officers, accompanied by the National Guard, stampeded into Short Creek. This polygamous community straddled the state line between Arizona and Utah—a strategic decision by FLDS leaders who settled in the isolated area in the 1930s when the mainstream LDS began cracking down on plural marriage. "Operation Seagull" was the brainchild of Arizona governor Howard Pyle, who arranged the police presence for that Sunday morning as well as busloads of social workers. The raid was not particularly a well-kept secret—Pyle was a politician, after all—so of course journalists and photographers joined the massive entourage.

Knowing the raid was coming, the brethren had told all the married men to congregate at the schoolhouse to sing hymns and pray. They didn't want the men caught in their homes with their multiple wives where relationships could be established. In the pre-dawn hours of July 26, 1953, civil authorities arrived with warrants for the arrest of thirty-five men. They arrested most of the adult male population of Short Creek and took

263 children as wards of the state. Father was at the schoolhouse when the raid took place and was arrested with all the men who gathered there. They were bussed over four hundred miles away to Kingman, Arizona—the Mohave County seat—to await trial.

After two and a half years of legal spatting, some of that time spent in jail or without their families, the men were given a slap on the wrist and forced to sign an agreement not to go back to their plural wives and children. This was a promise they didn't mind making, because they had no intention of honoring it. They simply moved their plural wives far enough away that authorities wouldn't be suspicious and continued to live the principle of plural marriage covertly. Father moved his family out of Short Creek north to the Salt Lake Valley, and for a few years his wives lived in separate residences but were still all married to Clyde Mackert Sr.

The memory of the raid was embedded in our souls, even for those of us who had not been born yet when it happened. Throughout my childhood, from the pulpit our leaders triumphantly remembered the "Raid of '53." Those who lived through it recounted how God had preserved our people. The media coverage worked to our advantage; newspapers published photos of crying babies being pulled from their fathers' arms, and the American people responded with sympathy and compassion for innocent families torn apart. Headlines around the country ridiculed the raid, and the political backlash was fierce. Governor Howard Pyle bore the weight of it and was never again elected to public office. The Saints rejoiced that God had created a political climate where government officials would think twice about ever coming after the FLDS again.

A few years later, the community changed its name to deflect ongoing publicity. Short Creek was divided into Colorado City, Arizona, and Hildale, Utah, but still functioned as one community. The population lived in a state of uneasy peace. Despite the victorious oratory of the leaders, the community inculcated an understanding that if we kept a low enough profile, we would be free to practice our religion without prosecution for violating state law.

KEEPING A low profile for a fundamentalist Mormon is like asking a leopard not to show its spots. The rigid dress code, particularly for women, made it easy to tell who was a fundamentalist and who wasn't, even in regions that were overwhelmingly Mormon. If a man was a wealthy fundamentalist in a nice, well-fitting suit, you couldn't tell him from a mainstream Mormon—unless he had one of his wives with him. The women were dead giveaways; their high collars, long sleeves, and dirt-dragging hemlines meant they could never be mistaken for anything but what they were. The only solution to this was to keep the women out of the public eye, which only increased the pervasive isolationism of the FLDS.

Some of the fundamentalists in our community had been devout mainstream LDS members who converted to living "the principle of plural marriage," along with other early doctrines of the LDS Church no longer at the forefront of LDS teachings. However, most of the fundamentalists were fifth-, sixth-, and seventh-generation polygamous Mormons—like me. All of the long-term fundamentalists had family stories of bravery and fortitude from the Mormon pioneer days of the LDS Church. Some accounts even went back to the life and times of Joseph Smith, the founder of the Mormon faith. Some claimed family members who fought against the Missouri mobs that rose up to drive the Mormons from the state during the Mormon-Missouri War of 1838. However, few could "boast" their fourth great-grandfather personally had a hand in establishing plural marriage. But I could.

My fourth great-grandfather was Isaac Allred, a member of the first High Council when Hyrum Smith presented, on his brother Joseph's behalf, what he claimed was a revelation from God that among other things justified plural marriage. It also claimed that those who lived according to this revelation would go to the highest degree of the celestial kingdom and become gods, priests, and rulers of men of their own worlds. Isaac Allred was one of nine council members who voted in favor of accepting this particular revelation, paving the way to incorporate it thirty years later (in 1873) as Section 132 of the *Doctrine and Covenants*—the scriptural canon of the LDS movement that is open to revision through revelation from God. So from its official inception in 1843, polygamy has been a part of my family.

I can also claim family ties to the Mormon-Missouri War, which in reality was a few skirmishes between Missouri residents and Mormons who had established Far West, Missouri, as their headquarters. Isaac Allred's eighteen-year-old son, William Moore Allred, represented our family as part of the Mormon militia raised to defend the Saints at Far West. The skirmishes culminated in the Battle of Crooked River, a stand-off between the Missouri state militia and the Mormons. In the end, Joseph Smith surrendered, and the Saints were expelled from the state of Missouri. Smith was taken as a prisoner to Independence, Missouri, but later escaped and rejoined the Saints in Nauvoo, Illinois, where the Mormons had regrouped.

William Moore Allred was also there when the Temple was later built in Nauvoo. In fact, he loaded the first wagonload of stones destined for the Nauvoo Temple, but a man who had a team of horses overtook William's slower oxen, and as a result, William missed the

honor of having his wagonload of stones be the first ones used in building the Temple.

After Joseph Smith's murder at the hands of an angry mob in 1844,
the Church was divided on the issue of plural marriage. Smith's wife,
Emma Hale Smith, denied there was any such thing as plural marriage,
despite evidence that Joseph Smith had thirty-three other wives. Ten
of these were teens when they married him; others were women who
had living husbands. Smith had lied about his teaching and practicing polygamy, and had even begun the practice before he received the
revelation in 1843 that stated a man must enter into plural marriage if
he wanted to progress to godhood and celestial exaltation. But Emma
Smith would have none of it and did not believe polygamy had a part
in the Mormon faith.

Others disagreed. Brigham Young and other early Mormon leaders were convinced they should seek out a place to live where they
could practice plural marriage. Those who sided with Emma Smith in
denouncing plural marriage remained in Nauvoo, Illinois. Those who
followed the Apostles who embraced the principle of plural marriage
left Nauvoo and headed westward, seeking asylum from the authority
of U.S. anti-polygamy laws in Utah, which belonged to Mexico at the
time. All the key leaders who went with Brigham Young were polygamists. The original Mormon teaching was that even God has a plurality
of wives, so if men want to be gods, they must have multiple wives as
well. These women were given to men to reproduce and create a kingdom, over which the man would be the god in the afterlife.

When the Saints headed west, they gathered on the shores of the
Missouri River to wait out the winter and prepare for the trek to Utah.
Making the journey westward would have been suicide in the winter,
especially considering how ill-prepared they really were. The place

where they waited became known as "Winter Quarters" and is located in what is now Omaha, Nebraska, and Council Bluffs, Iowa. William Moore Allred, my ancestor, built a wagon to carry his family but was unable to leave with the first wave for Utah because of the birth of his son Byron Harvey Allred, one of only three babies who survived being born into the harsh living conditions of Winter Quarters.

Brigham Young and his advance company proceeded on to the west after advising the remaining body of Saints to stay where they were in Indian Territory and to provide for themselves. In 1848, James Allred and his family continued with a one-hundred-wagon train, many of them Allreds, on their journey to Salt Lake City, Utah. However, Isaac Allred, along with other selected brethren, accompanied Young. On July 24, 1847, Young and his advance company entered the Salt Lake Valley.

The freedoms the Saints experienced in Utah were short-lived. The United States gained control of the region after the Mexican War, and it became the Utah Territory in 1850. The Mormons were no longer outside the reach of the U.S. government, and because of the continental expansion of the nation, they really had nowhere else to go. The government stepped up pressure to bring the Mormons into submission to its laws. President Buchanan even replaced Brigham Young with Alfred Cumming as the territorial governor in 1852 in order to establish U.S. supremacy over the territory. In 1887, Congress passed the Edmunds-Tucker Act, which outlawed polygamy within the Union. Federal marshals were dispatched to the Utah Territory to enforce new laws. As a result, LDS leaders were now on the run from the law.

On September 27, 1886, the president and Prophet of the LDS Church, John Taylor, claimed to have received a revelation from God while in hiding from federal marshals. The revelation was not published due to the circumstances of the times; however, it stated that plural marriage should never be relinquished. Immediately following this revelation, John Taylor called together a meeting that took place in the home of John W. Woolley. According to various accounts, five men were given the sealing authority to perform plural marriage and keep the principle alive by ensuring a child was born into it every year.

Wilford Woodruff succeeded John Taylor as the next president of the LDS Church in 1889. Woodruff inherited a church under pressure from the U.S. government, and to increase that pressure, the U.S. Supreme Court upheld the Edmunds-Tucker Act in 1890. With the Mormons' only hope for a legal solution to their troubles gone, Woodruff signed the "Manifesto," which officially stated that the LDS Church no longer taught or practiced plural marriage or polygamy. However, two days before presenting it for ratification at the general conference of the church, Woodruff summoned Byron Harvey Allred (my great-great-grandfather, born at Winter Quarters). According to Byron Harvey's journal entry, President Woodruff made no mention of a revelation from God concerning the Manifesto. President Woodruff only explained that the government would have seized all church property, including the Temple, if he had not signed the Manifesto. The work being performed in the Temple would have ended, and the leaders of the church would have been imprisoned for life. So Woodruff signed the Manifesto as a last resort, but it was really an empty gesture. He and other leaders had no intent in living out the policy. In fact, the purpose of the meeting with Byron Harvey and others was to dispatch them to Mexico, where polygamy was not against the law and would be out of the reaches of the U.S. government. Byron Harvey was to assist in establishing a colony in Mexico where plural marriage could be practiced. It was from covert actions such as this by LDS leaders that the fundamentalist Mormon strain was conceived.

In 1903, while living in the colony in Mexico, my great-grandfather Byron Harvey Allred Jr. was sealed to his first plural wife. This marriage took place more than thirteen years after Wilford Woodruff signed the Manifesto supposedly outlawing such practices. Anthony Ivins, who as stake president oversaw a number of Mormon groups, conducted the ceremony. Rather than being reprimanded for defying the Manifesto, Ivins was actually promoted to the status of Apostle for his work in Mexico to keep plural marriage alive. Because of events like this, it is obvious that the Manifesto was nothing more than a smokescreen created to deceive the U.S. government while polygamy flourished underground.

Times changed, though, and even the LDS Church began cracking down on the practice of polygamy beginning around the 1930s. Yet some insisted it was necessary according to the Mormon scriptures. The key question was *Who is following the teachings of Joseph Smith more faithfully: the LDS Church that has abandoned polygamy, or the splinter groups that have continued the practice?* The FLDS Church in which I grew up answered that question by saying they were following Smith's teachings, and the LDS Church had apostatized (fallen away from the truth) to appease the government. Through the decades, a hundred or so groups have split off from the LDS Church over this issue. Some form polygamous communities; some are families quietly living the principle of plural marriage without drawing attention to themselves. By the 1960s, when I was born, the fundamentalists were a constant reminder of a belief and practice that LDS leaders preferred to see fade into oblivion. One spin on it was that the practice had been a sort of social welfare system to take care of widows, though census records of the early decades of the Utah Territory show no record of a surplus of females.

In the 1930s, when the LDS Church began excommunicating members known to be living the principle of plural marriage, my great-grandfather Byron Harvey Allred Jr. wrote a book that critically analyzed the apostasy of the LDS Church from the original teachings set forth in the era of Joseph Smith and Brigham Young, who had set out to restore true Christian doctrine. His book, *A Leaf in Review,* is considered a must-have among fundamentalist Mormons.

So, according to all pre-Manifesto leaders of the LDS Church, only one path led to godhood, and that was through living the new and ever-lasting covenant of marriage. Plural marriage and the new and everlasting covenant were synonymous. From the ranks of those who continued to follow the principle of plural marriage came a group that banded together under the leadership of John Y. Barlow and Leroy S. Johnson. They formed the town of Short Creek. John Y. Barlow died before I was born, but some of my earliest memories include President Leroy S. Johnson, known as "Uncle Roy," a title the whole community used as a sign of respect for our Prophet. I also remember several of the Priesthood Council: Carl Holm, Richard Jessop, Marion Hammon, Rulon Jeffs, Guy Messer, and Alma Timpson. These are the leaders who headed what is now known as the Fundamentalist Church of Jesus Christ of Latter Day Saints. They held the Keys of the Priesthood, giving them the authority to seal eternal marriages.

For a long time, contention embroiled the council. It concerned a revelation supposedly given to Wilford Woodruff about who could receive revelations and who couldn't. Most of the council believed any of the Apostles could receive revelations. Of course, they would consult with other Apostles to confirm the revelation, but they could all receive them. For instance, any of them could make decisions about who should marry whom. Organizationally, someone had to be the leader of the council—the Prophet—but he had no more authority to receive revelations than the others. Some of the Apostles, however, held to the one-man doctrine, meaning that only one man—the Prophet—could receive revelations. The other Apostles were essentially counselors, but the Prophet was not bound by their counsel. Woodruff, before becoming president himself, had challenged all the Apostles to exercise their role of receiving revelations, but some early Mormon history supported the one-man doctrine.

Uncle Roy lived for decades after John Y. Barlow died, enjoying unchallenged reverence as the FLDS Prophet. But his death in 1986 brought the end of a tenuous balance of power between him and the Apostles who believed differently about the one-man doctrine. Uncle Roy embraced the one-man doctrine and believed he was the one man who could receive revelations, and Rulon Jeffs agreed. Marion Hammon and Alma Timpson, the only other remaining Apostles, disagreed. When Uncle Roy died, Marion Hammon should have received the position as president of the FLDS because he was the next most senior Apostle. Rulon Jeffs was next in line after Hammon. But, Rulon managed to convince Uncle Roy to name him as the successor, because he shared Uncle Roy's view, and Hammon did not. Hammon and Timpson of course objected to the validity of Rulon's presidency. A deep divide cut through the FLDS, and it was not easy for people to admit they had doubts about which Apostle to follow. However, Rulon had extra ammunition: He controlled the United Effort Plan (UEP) trust, the financial arm of the FLDS with millions of dollars of assets. Rulon had the single-handed power to divest people of their homes and livelihood, and expel them from the community if they didn't see things his way. Intimidation went a long way in convincing people that he was the true Prophet, the one man to follow.

Marion Hammon and Alma Timpson eventually left with their followers and settled the community of polygamists now living in Centennial Park, Arizona, on the border of Utah and Arizona and just south of the twin towns of Colorado City, Arizona, and Hildale, Utah.

So there I sat in the office of a navy psychiatrist. I was at the end of my allotted time with the heritage I received from my mother's side of the family flashing through my mind: seven generations of faithful submission to the principle of plural marriage from its inception. My family could trace its lines back to the time of Joseph Smith and the revelation he received about celestial marriage. Seven generations of lives filled with chronic fear of exposure.

Who was I? No, this was not an easy question.

"My father is a polygamist Mormon," I blurted out. "He had four wives and thirty-one children. I am his twenty-eighth child, if you include stepchildren."

It took awhile for the shock to fade from his face, but eventually he resumed his professional composure.

"Of your mother's children, which one are you?" he asked. "And not counting the stepchildren, which one are you?"

"I am my mother's seventh and youngest child," I reported. I had to stop and think for a minute to answer the second question. "Well, without the stepchildren, Father had twenty-seven kids, and I was the fourth to last, so I guess I was number twenty-four of twenty-seven."

Laughing awkwardly, he asked, "Do you feel like a number?"

"Yes, I suppose I do. *'Number twenty-four, front and center,'*" I bellowed. "*'You're in big trouble now, number twenty-four!'*"

The laughter helped break the tension, and I began to feel more at ease. Somehow the doctor had acquired a warmer image than the iceberg I had originally assumed him to be. I wasn't quite so worried about being carted off in a straight jacket. I could see the familiar questions bobbing behind his eyes, though.

"I imagine that being one of the youngest of your father's children, your relationship with him wasn't very close," he said.

"That's putting it politely," I said. I hadn't expected anything to come out of this session, but the doctor had just cut to the heart of my pain. "My father was a convert, but he never had a close relationship with his own father, either. But how can a man with thirty-one children have time for all of them—or any of them?"

He nodded, so I continued, my voice rising to rant level.

"It's all about authority, just trying to keep the household from disintegrating into chaos. Relating to children is diminished to tactics used for breaking horses."

"Yes, but the new methodology in breaking horses isn't centered on domination, but a partnership with the horse," the doctor explained.

"Well, the FLDS does it the old-fashioned way, where you establish your dominance over your subject, whether it's a horse or a child. Once you have dominance, you have blind obedience."

"So your homicidal feelings toward your father are because he wasn't there for you, lacked good fathering skills, and established his dominance over you and your siblings." The doctor was trying to get his head around the complexities of my childhood.

I hesitated. "Those are factors in the equation, but not the reason."

And then the moment shattered. The next patient had arrived.

I couldn't believe it, but we were going to have to quit.

"I know we haven't gotten very far today," the doctor said, "but that's not what today was about. Today was about me getting to know you better. I want you to know I'm here for you. If you feel overwhelmed, just call the hospital and tell them you need to talk. We have counselors trained to help at all hours." He stepped in front of me to make sure he had my attention. "Even if you need to come and stay here for a few days and have some medication to calm you, that's better than doing something to hurt yourself or someone else. I don't want you to be afraid to avail yourself of our help. It won't get you locked up in a mental ward; it will only give you time to regain control and get you through this."

I believed him. I'd come a long way in my short time with him that day. I decided in that instant to trust him. I didn't know where all this would lead, but anywhere was better than where I was. Something had to change. Like the sailors of old who set out to sail past the edge of the world—fear of the unknown mingled with the excitement of something new.

But I walked out of his office knowing I still had not spoken aloud the reason I wanted to kill my father.

2

Ever Since I Was Little

And now a commandment I give unto you—if you will be
delivered you shall set in order your own house, for there
are many things that are not right in your house ... see
that they are more diligent and concerned at home, and
pray always, or they shall be removed out of their place.

—*Doctrine and Covenants, Section 93:43, 50*

A week later I returned to Balboa Naval Hospital for my second
appointment with my psychiatrist. Would this be the day I revealed
the whole truth?

On the drive out to the hospital, the notion attacked me that the
psychiatrist might have called in sick or decided that on a beautiful San
Diego day he would rather be golfing than tending to needy patients. It
was irrational, but I was on the verge of convincing myself he would leave
me in the hands of an intern while he hit the sunny links. So when he was
actually there at the appointed hour, I was so relieved that I welcomed his
warm greeting.

"Hello, Brian. How was your week?"

"It was all right, I suppose. I haven't killed anyone or myself, haven't been in any fights, and didn't drink with the exception of the weekend— which I don't remember because I was drunk. In other words, it was a typical week for any sailor, except that most sailors would have been in at least one fight."

He let go of a laugh. "Good to see you haven't lost your sense of humor," he said. "So you haven't been entertaining thoughts of killing your father, then?"

"It wasn't that good of a week," I responded. "I've thought about it, but in the end I resigned myself to the idea that thoughts like that might become a thing of the past if I gave it some time."

"Good. That's a healthy way to look at it," he said. "No thoughts about hurting yourself, either?"

"No, I don't think I have the courage it would take to do something like that."

"Good." He paused to offer hospitality. "Would you like some water, coffee, or tea?"

"Water would be nice," I said, not realizing I was launching a habit that would characterize our meetings.

He asked his receptionist to bring me a glass of water, and I took my place in the chair opposite his desk. "While we're waiting for your water, I want you to think back on some of your earliest recollections as a child. What are some of the first things you can remember?"

My water arrived, and I sipped it as I pondered his question. I knew a lot of stories about my early childhood, but how many of them did I remember, and how many had been repeated to me enough times that I knew the details? And, of course, I knew a lot of stories about my large family even from the time before I was born.

Shortly after I became the latest addition to my father's clan, most of the family was finally living under one roof, following a history of multiple locations. Mother Midge, my father's first wife, had lived in LaSalle and Moab, Utah, with her children after the raid of 1953, and then moved back to Colorado City, Arizona. Mother Donna and my own mother, Myra, had also moved around a lot within the Salt Lake Valley. Eventually, Mother Midge lived in Taylorsville, Mother Donna lived in West Jordan, and Mom lived in Kearns—all in the Salt Lake Valley. Mom would take her kids over to Mother Donna's while she went to work. The goal was always to live together in one household. For a while, these three wives and their children did live together in a house in the "Avenues" of North Salt Lake City. I don't remember much about that house because I was a preschooler when we moved out of it, but my older siblings sure do. Gather them around a table and just say "the house in the Aves," and you will be entertained for hours listening to the stories they tell of life inside that house. The same is true of the other houses. I remember stories told to me about events that happened before I was old enough to remember them myself.

Kids are kids. They're going to get into mischief. By the time I was born, my oldest siblings were in their twenties, so never did all thirty-one children live together at once. But there were always a lot of kids, and that magnified the degree of our adventures. Even in a household characterized by strict discipline and harsh expectations, kids found ways to be kids.

My older siblings had a propensity toward practical jokes. The worst possible scenario was for siblings to discover something they could use against you. Any quirks in your character were fair game—especially if you were younger than the prankster. Dominance was the name of the game. Older kids let younger ones know who was in charge, and younger ones strove to prove they were grown up. Perhaps this is not so unusual in sibling relationships, but multiply by the scale of a polygamous household and it's a whole new ball game. Even as a toddler, I was not exempt from the pranks my siblings would play for the sake of their own entertainment—and because they could.

I was a plump and juicy toddler, with fat rings around my wrists and any other places that could bend. Unfortunately for me, my siblings discovered I was terrified of the doorbell, and this was too tempting of an opportunity. Our doorbell in those days was a smaller version of the old-fashioned fire alarms, with a round bell and hammer connected to an electric motor that would cause the hammer to repeatedly beat against the bell. My siblings took exquisite joy in starting a game of chase that would take my path right past the front door, and when the time was right, one sibling would signal to another to ring the bell—and scare the living daylights out of me. My siblings loved to see how fast I could move my fat little legs. This was a source of laughter on many days.

When I want to, I can really rub it in my sisters' faces that they didn't do a good job looking after me. When we lived in Kearns, Utah, one of their favorite games involved bouncing me on a bed. Sitting on the bed, they would slap their hands on the bed twice, then throw their heads back and bounce on the mattress and come right back up. As a toddler, I thought this was extremely funny and quickly learned to do it. Unfortunately one time they didn't notice that I had worked my way to the edge of the bed. When I slapped my hands and threw my head back, I flipped right off the bed. When Mom arrived home later, I was still very fussy. She thought I had an earache because I kept pawing at my head behind my right ear.

The next day, Mom went to work, and Mother Donna stayed home with the kids, as usual. At about 10:00, Mother Donna called Mom. "Myra, are you sitting down?"

"Yes?"

"Don't panic, but something's wrong with Brian. It feels like his skull has been crushed."

Of course, this sent Mom into a state of mild hysteria. She scrambled home and whisked me off to the doctor, who drained the fluid that had collected between my skull and scalp—directly behind my right ear.

When I tell this story now, I always point out the poor babysitting skills of my older siblings who neglected to keep me out of harm's way. I ask my sisters' children, "Have they dropped you on your head yet?"

I had innumerable other mishaps as a small child that have turned into family stories. A metal door in one house sliced a piece off the end of one finger, and a doctor had to stitch it back together. Another time, I wandered down the street, and no one noticed until a policeman found me with a quite protective family dog and took me home.

NONE OF these stories were my own memories, though; they were family lore. I thought long and hard about the doctor's question of my earliest memories. The furthest back I could recall was when I was four, and we were preparing to move into the big house in Sandy, Utah, just south of Salt Lake City. The move there was designed to bring all of Father's families together under one roof permanently. The big house in Sandy became the most stable living environment our family would ever know.

The house was located just off State Street. The address is burned into my memory: 113 East 9730 South, Sandy, Utah 84070. The property was shaped like a long rectangle and dissected along its length by a road. The previous owner had given the right of way to the city to put a road through running from east to west, but our land spanned both the north and south sides. We dubbed the road "Our Road" because we owned the land on both sides of it for more than 60 percent of its length. Funny, though, that name never caught on at city hall, where it remained 9730 South. Our big house is gone now, and the new Jordan High School stands where the house once stood.

To the west of us was Johanna's Café, situated where our road ended in a "T" intersection with State Street. It sat at the top of a long hill sloping down toward the city of Draper to the south. Across from the café was Wyllie's Welding Shop, and on one side Mr. Hyde's Gas Station and Garage. His junkyard became one of my favorite playgrounds because our land adjoined the fence to his property.

When we moved in, there was nothing but open fields in all directions except the west. On the eastern boundary of our land a railroad track rumbled north and south. Beyond the tracks open fields rolled all the way to the foothills of the mountains to the east. A small grove of trees lined the western side of the railroad tracks just north of our property, providing shade from summer sun and an intriguing place to play. To the south were open fields owned by a man named Johnny Cole, who grazed several hundred head of cattle there. A canal wound its way through his field. Further south was a gully that had an old abandoned cement factory in it.

The best way to stay out of trouble was to stay out of the house and play outside during the day. The house and barn were located on the western third of the property, and the other two-thirds were open pastures available for whatever we could manage to do with them.

It was here in Sandy that I came to understand just how large Father's family was. I had always known Mother Midge, Mother Donna, and Mom. But, when we prepared to move into the Sandy house, another woman appeared with some new children. I was only four years old at the time, so I didn't understood that Father had yet another wife, Mother Maurine. Much later I learned that they had met in a bar and married. Maurine had four children from a previous marriage, and the five of them now joined the rest of the family.

As a four-year-old, it all seemed perfectly natural. Father had four wives and we practiced polygamy, just like the biblical patriarchs. Abraham had two wives, and Jacob had two wives and two concubines. (Of course, I had no idea what a concubine was!) As a young child, I didn't know anything else but polygamous family life.

My father had not grown up in either the LDS or FLDS Church. As far as I know, neither he nor Midge had any particular religious background when they married. They hadn't been married long when they began to have marital troubles, and apparently my father was not entirely faithful when he served in the army in Puerto Rico. Around this time, some women who belonged to the FLDS Church befriended Midge. She read the *Book of Mormon* and decided she believed it, including plural marriage. When my father returned from Puerto Rico, Midge told him that if he wanted to see her or their twin daughters again, he should agree to become a polygamous Mormon. Midge was giving Father his cake and letting him eat it too! He agreed to join the FLDS Church and take additional wives—with Midge's encouragement at the time.

Father and Midge had eleven children: twins Connie and Carole, Lucy, Clyde Jr., Phil, Paula, Howard, Roberta, Stan, Andrea, and Camille.

Father's second wife was Mother Donna. Mother Donna and my mom were sisters, which meant that Mother Donna's children were not only my half siblings, but also my first cousins. Throwing around statements like that can leave people dazed, confused, and pondering what the gene pool must be like. I assure you, there was no inbreeding in anything I've described. Actually, the situation was quite like Jacob's dilemma in Genesis 29. Jacob wanted to marry Rachel, but her father tricked him into first marrying her older sister, Leah. So some of Jacob's children found themselves in the same situation as I was, with half siblings who were also cousins. My father wanted to marry my mother, Myra, but the Priesthood Council—the ultimate authority in the FLDS—insisted that her older sister Donna must be married first. At least that's the way Mom tells it. Donna's children were Seth, Charlotte, Shem, Karen, Stephen, Kenneth, Mark, Maria, and Melanie.

My mother, Myra, was Father's third wife. My full siblings are Mary, Rowena (Rena), David, Kathleen, Paul, and Laura. I am the youngest of my mother's children, though some of Mother Donna's children are younger than I am.

Father's fourth wife was Mother Maurine. Her four children—Daniel, Tori, John, and Doreen—were from a previous marriage and bore the family name Swaney.

Now obviously all of these people were not going to fit into one house. Many of the older ones were already married off by the time we moved to Sandy: Connie, Carole, Lucy, Clyde, Seth, Charlotte, and Mary. But even without making room for these siblings, at one point we still had twenty-four children and five parents living under one roof.

Working on the house is one of the clearest early memories I have. When Father purchased the property, it had only a cramped cinderblock house on it. There wasn't much to be done with this house because it didn't have enough space for anything; the land was what Father wanted. He then purchased an old office building scheduled to be torn down and had it moved to the property onto a new foundation. This could be converted into a giant house that would be big enough for all of us. We put the house on the north side of the property, across the street from the cinderblock house. The foundation was poured so that the house would sit at a forty-five degree angle to the street, which shielded our backyard from view.

My brother Mark and I were terribly excited about all this commotion, even though we were only four. I remember the house had been set on the foundation, which was a half-basement foundation where the window seals are just above ground level. To make the office building more houselike, the plan called for replacing the flat roof with a pitched roof. The older boys were working feverishly at putting the trusses on the house, and Mark and I were deposited in a pile of sand on the other side of the dirt road. Father wanted to keep us a safe distance from the construction. We played in the sand awhile, but what was happening on the construction side of the road looked so much more enticing. It was only a matter of time before we were scampering around the site trying to hand tools to people who didn't need them or provide some other service we had deemed useful.

"Brian! Mark! What on God's green earth are you doing over here?" Father bellowed. "Kenneth, take Brian and Mark back across the street to the pile of sand and get them interested in something."

Eight-year-old Ken obediently took Mark and me by the hands and led us back across the street. He played there with us for a few minutes, filling a Tonka truck with sand and dumping it where we directed him. When Ken thought it safe, he resumed his place among the ranks of the older boys in the building effort. The sand pile simply could not compete, and before long Mark and I ambled across the road again. At first we took refuge behind our mothers and sisters who were watching the construction process from a safe distance. But gradually we made our way unnoticed back into the fray of things and once again set about offering our services.

Unexpectedly, a board fell from my brother Shem's hands and slammed down on the floor next to my feet. Suddenly Shem realized I was there and yelled at me to get out of the way.

This pattern repeated several times—we were sent across the street but managed to return to the worksite and escape notice for a while. Eventually, Father discovered us yet again, and this time he'd had enough. He snatched us up by our wrists and carried us across the street. He gripped both our wrists in one massive hand and with his free hand pulled a wooden stake out of the ground, without breaking stride. He paddled our backsides with that stake the rest of the way to the sand pile, telling us it was for our own good and "this hurts me more than it hurts you." Mark and I were crying buckets by then, but Father didn't look like it was hurting him one bit. We concluded the real danger lay in what Father would do to us if we crossed the road again, rather than any construction accident.

That is my first real memory: being harshly disciplined by a father who generally had no time for me. As I grew older, I realized this was not just because I had been a disobedient four-year-old. Father rarely spoke to me, seldom touched me, and almost never looked me in the eyes.

It wasn't long before the house was remodeled enough to move in. It had twenty-two bedrooms and eight bathrooms. Upstairs was a living room, dining room, kitchen, Father's study, Father's bedroom and bathroom, a separate bed and bath combo for each mother, and nurseries for children who might yet be born. Downstairs was where the real action was. The laundry room held multiple washers and dryers, and the basement boasted two recreation rooms where we could hang out and amuse ourselves. One end of the basement was the boys' end and the other the girls' end. Both areas had multiple bedrooms and bathrooms. Mark and I shared a room for most of my life in the big house in Sandy.

Under Mother Donna's near-militaristic rule, the labor in the house was divided into regimented chores for boys and chores for girls. The girls took care of the cooking and cleaning, and the boys took care of the gardens and livestock. Father had purchased a beef cow and a milk cow to start us off in providing both beef and milk. The beef cow we named Esmerelda, fondly known as Ezie, and the milk cow we named Brown Sugar, affectionately called Sug. We had more of a hands-on relationship with Sug, for obvious reasons. Ezie we left alone except when it was time to have the vet come and inseminate her.

Occasionally, Johnny Cole's bull in the neighboring field would volunteer his services by breaking down the fence and fathering a calf. Keeping him out of our fields and away from our growing number of cattle was always a challenge. Many times we had to venture into his field to bring our cows home, or chase him out of our field, and then we had to mend the fence, which seemed to be a constant chore.

On the north half of the property where the main house stood, we sectioned off a portion of a pasture for our garden. We planted mostly corn, but we also had squash, cucumbers, carrots, radishes, tomatoes, and other common garden vegetables. It was our job as boys to keep the livestock—and the vermin—out of the garden, and also to irrigate the pastures and garden with water the city would channel to us through a network of irrigation ditches. In the north pasture was a pile of wood from the trees leveled when the previous owner cleared the property. We managed to burrow a hole into the center of the woodpile and create another fascinating place to play. The southern half of the pasture we left to the livestock because it was near the barn where we milked the cows.

We also had a pigpen and a barnyard with a chicken coop. All of these farm animals assisted in providing for our large family. We had fresh vegetables from the garden, as well as beef, pork, and chicken, not to mention the steady supply of milk and eggs. Father worked as a certified public accountant, and Mothers Midge, Myra, and Maurine all worked to help sustain the family. Mother Donna was the "at-home mom." Boys who were over sixteen years old and could legally work gave their paychecks to Father. Those who were under the age of sixteen worked for companies owned and operated by other polygamists. For example, some of my siblings worked in Rulon Jeffs's jewelry-making business located in the back half of Johanna's Café, just down the road.

We were all together, all the mothers and my father living under one roof. We had the true faith, and we lived separate from the apostates and heathens of the world so we would not bring sin on ourselves. This is where I grew up: a huge family; a wonderland of property; barnyard animals to care for, love on, and learn from; and brothers to cavort with. It was here I would learn to rope, ride, milk cows, mend fences, and get into plenty of childhood trouble. Looking back, this is always the place that comes to mind if someone asks me where I'm from. This was the place I called home. What more could a boy want?

Yet something was missing. Something was not right. This was also the place I would learn to deceive and turn my head when something didn't add up. This was the place I would cower in my own father's presence. This was the place I would fight to make somebody—anybody—notice me and tell me I mattered.

❖ ❖ ❖

When the doctor asked me about my earliest memories, so much flooded through my mind. However, I knew the place to start was that farm in Sandy. And I knew I could not tell much more of the story without revealing the reason for my rage against my father.

3

Life on the Farm

*But behold, I say unto you, that little children ... cannot
sin, for power is not given unto Satan to tempt little
children, until they begin to become accountable before
me; for it is given unto them even as I will ... that great
things may be required at the hand of their fathers.*

—*Doctrine and Covenants, Section 29:46–48*

I got plenty of dishwashers right here."

That was Father's answer to the notion that perhaps we needed
an automatic dishwasher—or three. And that was generally the answer to
everything that had to be done around the farm. Life on the farm was like
running a small business enterprise, and the kids were the free labor.

Mother Donna had her hands full taking care of all the children
while the other mothers worked. However, she had at her disposal
the FLDS culture of hierarchy and dominance, a useful tool to keep
everyone in line. The older the sibling, the more rank he or she held in
governing the home. If you disobeyed older siblings, they only had to

report your behavior to Mother Donna and you were in deep trouble. Mother Donna grew up in the age of corporal punishment, when children were sent out to acquire the instrument of their own castigation at the nearby willow tree. Occasionally, if she feared a child would take too long selecting a discipline device, a wire coat hanger came in handy. Nothing was more frightful than hearing the whisk of a willow strap or coat hanger as it cut through the air just prior to smacking the intended target. The resulting welts served as a continuing reminder of the infraction. Once, I couldn't sit down for a week, literally.

Mother Donna always had something for us to do, and sometimes keeping all of those kids in line meant acting like a military officer more than a mother. After all, despite the title of "Mother" Donna, most of us were not her kids, but she was charged with the job of raising us nevertheless. Being the children of Clyde Mackert bound us together, but he wasn't interested in the daily interactions of the household. That was Mother Donna's territory. When he came home from work, he didn't have anything to say to us—and if he did, we were petrified what it might be. Mostly we just tried to stay out of his way while he plopped down in front of the TV and ignored us. Those TV images of families glad to have their dads home after work were nothing like our life. But, of course, we weren't supposed to be watching TV with all its worldliness, and we weren't supposed to talk about Father's TV habits. The mood of the house changed when Father came home. Laughter ceased; children scattered. The place to be was beyond Father's line of sight. Sometimes Father's glance lingered on my sisters but never me. I remember Kathleen would hide under a table when Father came home from work. I didn't understand the reasons until much later. A lot of us wanted to stay out of sight and under the table was as good a place as any.

I didn't always know what we were afraid of when it came right down to it. When I was little, I saw the fear in my siblings' eyes and followed their example—apparently we were supposed to be afraid of Father. I did know that if we acted out to the point that Mother Donna reported us to Father, that was serious business. My father was my priesthood head; if I wasn't right with Father, I couldn't be right with God, and if I wasn't right with God, I couldn't become a god myself. Accountability weighed heavily on us from the time we learned right from wrong and was hammered into us at every opportunity. But I also wanted my father to come to the dinner table. I wanted him to ask what I learned in school. I wanted him to look at me and see me sitting there. Why was the TV always more important than I was? Of course, I could never tell him how I felt; that wasn't the FLDS way.

Being the youngest boys, Mark and I wanted badly to learn to do everything the older boys did. Father was never around to demonstrate the skills we needed in order to participate in farm work, so we were left to the mercies of our older brothers, who might or might not decide we were worthy of learning. Brothers Clyde, Seth, and Phillip were married or off on work missions in Colorado City, Arizona. David, Howard, and Shem were all working for Apostle Marion Hammon on his farms in Idaho and Colorado City. So, on the farm, Steve, Stan, Paul, and Ken were the boys in the know, and Mark and I were the wannabees.

When it was time for the nightly milking and feeding, Mark and I would scamper out to the barn and watch Steve, Stan, Paul, and Ken as they brought in Sugar for her milking, and later the other cows as the herd grew. But milking a cow was not something little boys could jump into. We had to work ourselves up the ladder of chores to be considered trustworthy enough to milk the cows. Like all little boys, we just wanted to be big boys. In our case, we had to depend on our brothers to teach us what we needed to know.

The first thing Mark and I had to learn to do was feed the calves. Eventually, we also were allowed to learn how to bring the cows down from the top of the pasture. One day, Sugar refused to come down from the pasture. Stan, who was the top dog in chore assignments, instructed Ken to take Mark and me up to the pasture to fetch Sugar.

"Sugar isn't your average cow," Ken informed us authoritatively on the way to the pasture. Mark and I knew that already, but, of course, we wouldn't interrupt Ken when we were trying to acquire his secret knowledge. "She sometimes gets blue and feels neglected. She only wants someone to come up here and pay attention to her."

I certainly knew that feeling. If Sugar was half as lonely inside as I was, I felt sorry for her.

"When we get close to her," Ken continued, "don't do anything stupid. Just watch me. When I start scratching her under the chin, you come and do the same thing. Tell her what a wonderful cow she is; tell her she's a good mama."

How could Sugar not like this attention? I sure would have.

Ken's final instructions came. "When I turn to walk down the pasture, you turn and walk with me. Don't look back. She'll follow us down."

This I had to see. As much as I respected Ken's experience and authority, somehow I had trouble believing this theory.

Ken walked up to Sugar just as casually as could be. Sugar lifted her head and took in a deep whiff of Ken's scent as he slid his hands under her chin and began scratching. We followed instructions and also scratched the cow, heaping accolades about her maternal virtues. Finally Ken turned away and started strolling back to the barn.

"How do we know she'll follow?" I couldn't help asking. I had to know!

"Trust me. She'll follow."

Mark asked, "What if we get all the way to the barn and she hasn't followed?"

The words had barely escaped Mark's lips when the answer came. He was suddenly lifted off the ground by a mysterious force behind him.

"Hey!" he exclaimed as he thudded back to earth.

Sugar came to a stop, looking away as if she hadn't seen a thing, much less perpetrated anything.

Ken burst out laughing. "That's how you know."

At Mark's expense, we learned that Sugar responded to a little affection and encouragement. As young as I was, I was slightly envious of a cow. Affection and encouragement sounded plenty good to me.

Mark and I hoped that soon the older boys would consider us worthy to learn to actually milk a cow. We were diligent about executing our chores properly so we'd be ready to move up the chore ladder.

"Have you fed the cows their hay and watered them?" Steve asked us one day when we were about seven.

"Yes!" we responded.

"Have you slopped the pigs?"

"Yes!"

"Did you feed the chickens and gather the eggs?"

"Yes!" We were grinning by this time, because we knew where this was heading. The day had come.

"Well, then," Steve said, "come and sit next to me, and I'll show you how to milk a cow." Steve assigned Paul to demonstrate for me, while he showed Mark himself.

Paul motioned me over with a swing of his head and pointed to an old cinderblock. "Use that as a stool."

Eagerly, I grabbed the cinderblock and set it on end, all the while listening intently to Paul. I didn't want to miss a word. He explained the bucket of warm water we brought from the house to clean the udder before milking. He showed me where to place the milk bucket and how to hold it in place with my knee so the cow couldn't kick it. I learned to clinch the cow's tail between my thigh and calf to keep it from whipping my face. I experimented with leaning my forehead into the cow's flank so I could detect a warning if she was going to shift her weight.

From there, the lesson proceeded to the technique of grasping teats and developing a rhythm of pulling. Paul demonstrated slowly at first so I could see clearly. A white stream of steamy milk splashed into the bottom of the bucket. Paul picked up his pace, going faster and faster until he was in his normal rhythm. Finally, Paul told me I could take my stool to the other side of the cow and begin working on the two teats on the other side. The moment had come: I was allowed to milk Sugar, the family's favorite cow! Before long, Mark and I were just as efficient as the older boys, and milking was a regular part of our routine.

One winter morning when I was about twelve, something was wrong with Sugar. She wouldn't eat and acted sick. Her milk had completely dried up after providing for us for years. When the veterinarian came to examine her, he discovered she had swallowed a baling wire. He gave her a magnet to swallow in hopes that it would catch the wire and help her pass it. After he was gone, we carefully monitored her condition, vigilant for any sign of improvement. But one morning about two weeks later when Mark and I went out to do the milking, we saw Sugar lying on her side. As soon as we saw her, we knew she was dead. We ran up to her to check, but we couldn't see any breath in the cold air and she was cold to the touch.

I muddled through my chores, then broke the news to the family. I was not unfamiliar with the passing of animals; we lived on a farm, after all. But losing Sugar was different. In the privacy of my room, where no one could see what I was feeling, I cried for the cow I had envied, the cow who had demanded affection from time to time. Now there was no living creature left who understood how I felt.

GARDENING WAS another incessant chore. We had to weed, of course, but the big job was irrigating both the garden and the pastures, because the water didn't come to us; we had to go get it. The city of Sandy deserved its name because of its arid environment; however, its network of irrigation ditches, which spread out the precious water, kept the land lush and green. The water was rationed with biweekly time slots allotted for the occupants to flood their fields. For us, getting water meant going upstream and turning the gates that would redirect water from our upstream neighbor to our land. Sometimes this consisted simply of walking up a field or two from ours and turning a gate. Sometimes, however, the neighbor had not bothered to access the water, and we had to travel further to turn other gates to guide the water flow in our direction. It could be a bit of a hunt to find where the water had last stopped. The city rationing also meant that our turn would arise at various times of day, so occasionally we had to start the water flow in the middle of the night.

Once we found the water and turned it toward the ditches that would eventually lead to our pastures, we had some justification for hanging around the ditch. On hot summer days, nothing was more refreshing than "accidentally" slipping and falling into the water. My brothers grasped enough of the engineering principles to keep the water flowing sufficiently that we could even float some of the way. Of course, we weren't supposed to be doing that. Swimming was strictly forbidden, so engaging in this behavior required willful, premeditated disobedience. We manufactured an assortment of cover stories: sliding into the water while clearing a jam, or rescuing a young bird that had fallen from its nest and landed in the ditch, or blaming one boy for pushing someone in and instigating a water fight—in which we naturally had to participate to save our honor against such an insult.

Mark and I learned a lot of lessons from our brothers about taking care of livestock and grown-up responsibilities. But the biggest lesson we learned was how to deceive our parents in a systematic way. It didn't feel at all unnatural, since so much of our polygamous life was based on deceit and convoluted explanations. We had plenty of models from people in authority for how to pull this off. We'd been carefully indoctrinated in the stories to tell under particular circumstances even though we knew they weren't true. All of those times we were taught how to lie to protect the family and our father's identity—what was the difference if we made up stories to cover our fun?

SUMMERS OFFERED almost unending opportunities for getting into mischief and hiding much of what we were doing from our parents. Mother Donna would quickly tire of a house full of kids who had no school and banish us to the great outdoors. The problem was there wasn't much we could do outside, either. Everything that was fun was also something that would get us in trouble. We couldn't swim because the water had been cursed and the devil had been given control over it. Anything in the water was also under the control of the devil, so just sticking your toe in meant you were putting yourself at the devil's mercy. At least that's what our parents said. We weren't allowed to have water fights even on the hottest day unless one of the mothers sanctioned the activity, which was rare. We couldn't play with neighbors because, well, we didn't have any neighbors to play with. The closest ones were all LDS Mormons, who were essentially Gentiles to us. So, naturally, having any fun required a great deal of planning and deception and was heavily rooted in the hierarchy of the children in the family.

The barn served as a great enabler for the boys. It was much more than a place to be rebellious against Father's rules; it was a place where we could be anything we wanted—a privilege we knew would never be part of our real life. We could be cowboys and Indians, we could be pirates, we could be anything our imaginations dreamed up. Our barn was my never-never land, where boys never grew up and anything was possible. Inside the barn, I played my first hand of poker—though cards were a tool of the devil. Inside the barn, I listened to my first rock 'n' roll song—music of the devil. Inside the barn I saw my first *Playboy,* smoked my first cigarette (which I stole from Father), and drank my first beer—all taboo, obviously. Did I know better? Yes. Did my brothers know better? Yes. All these behaviors were cursed. They were all flagrant violations of the laws for living handed down through the generations from Joseph Smith, and we all knew that if you didn't keep all the laws faithfully, you could not progress to godhood. As males, it was especially important that we progress to godhood.

We knew that in our heads. Apparently we didn't believe it. Or maybe we knew we had already sinned so much and we were already so unworthy that another day's adventure really didn't matter. Maybe we thought that if no one knew, the sin didn't count. Or maybe we were striving to find our own worthiness through the constant competitions that made up our play.

I LEARNED more about goofing off and getting away with it out there in that barn than I did anything else. When Mark and I first began going out to help milk the cows, my brothers protested. I didn't understand why at first, but I began to catch on. They didn't want us to know what they were doing out there so that we couldn't tell on them. When we were younger, they couldn't count on us to participate in the deceit. However, as we participated in more of their mischievous activities, they could trust us because if we were caught, we would be just as guilty as they were. They realized that if they let us have a look at a *Playboy*, we weren't going to tell on them for having it. If we tattled, our parents would surely inquire if we had looked at it as well, and if we answered truthfully, we'd incriminate ourselves. If we answered falsely, the other boys were sure to tell a different story in their own defense.

My brothers and I played with each other and with other boys from the church at a bloodthirsty, competitive level. We loved sports because it gave us something to do, but also because it gave us a chance to impress Father. He had been a boxer and football player in college—before his conversion to the FLDS—so we all learned to box and to play football, hoping to meet with his approval. You never knew who would show up to play, but it was a chance to see someone besides your own siblings outside of school, so we took advantage of it. During football season, we would all meet down at Jordan High School to play tackle football. The Jeffs boys would meet the Mackerts there, along with the Barlows and others, and we'd pick teams. Often the Mackerts outnumbered the others, so we'd play a game of the Mackerts against everyone else. In the summer, we'd play basketball or softball on Saturdays.

Father never came to watch us play, though, so that motive was in vain. Only one time, on a Thanksgiving Day, did he come. We were all pretty hyped to see him sitting there and determined to play the best game ever.

Five minutes later he was gone.

Father's absence did not erase our need for attention and acknowledgment. It just redirected things, especially for the younger boys. Since earning my father's approval was hopeless, I strove to obtain my brothers' approval by perfecting my skills at playing football. I practiced and practiced. Mark and I worked together on throwing and catching the ball, as well as learning how to take a hand-off, throw a lateral pass, and block.

I couldn't help but wish my father were around to see me play. I had a mental image of making a three-pointer on the basketball court or kicking an unbelievable field goal that wins the game. When that happens to a boy, the first person he wants to hug is his father. But I knew that could never be. Father was never there—but my brothers were.

One day my brother Steve lost it and started chewing out his offensive line and told them how deficient they were by acknowledging that I was putting out my best effort on every play. It didn't matter if I was double-teamed or advanced on by an older, bigger boy; I was going to pressure the quarterback into throwing the ball before he was ready to or taking the sack. And here was Steve acknowledging my effort and giving me credit in front of a bunch of other kids, many of them older than I was. That acknowledgment was momentous for me! I was worthy of Steve's acceptance. It was a thrill when my older brothers let me start playing tight-end, halfback, and quarterback because they knew I was good at football. After years of wondering, I mattered.

ONE DAY, Stan, Steve, Paul, and Ken assigned Mark and me to milk the cows on our own. They made a big deal out of this, so of course Mark and I jumped at the chance to prove that we could handle the job. What we didn't know was the plan our brothers had for the free time they had just carved out for themselves. At the haystack outside the barn, they had purposely arranged hay bales to create a hidden center room, complete with a bale rigged to function as a door—a perfect hiding place for several boys. Next, standing safely behind the haystack, my brothers waited in ambush for cars coming down our road to see if they could hit one with a snowball. Hitting a car moving at twenty-five to thirty-five miles per hour is not as easy as you might think. You didn't throw your ball at the car; you threw it where you thought the car would be when your snowball arrived. Needless to say, a great deal of trial and error was involved.

On this particular day, Stan happened to be extremely lucky. He successfully targeted a semi-tractor trailer. His shot actually went through the open window of the cab and hit the driver on the left side of the face! About six inches of snow on the ground had been packed down by passing cars. On this slick surface, the truck's brakes locked up and it started to jackknife, then straightened out and pulled off the road. Stan, Steve, Paul, and Ken all scrambled into the secret room in the middle of the haystack and closed the bale-door.

Inside the barn, Mark and I were peacefully milking cows, blissfully unaware of any of this. Suddenly an angry truck driver kicked in the door of the barn, spewing a murderous stream of profanities. I thought we were going to be killed, that this was some mad man who had roamed randomly into our barn intent on killing anyone in his path. With our stomachs in our throats, we jabbered and stammered and hoped we made some sense. We had nothing to do with the snowball that had found its way into his cab, we assured him. We showed him the amount of milk in our buckets and assured him we wouldn't have that much warm milk if we'd been out messing around with snowballs.

"If it wasn't you, then who was it?" he shouted. "The snowball came from this side of the road."

We shrugged and offered various explanations—kids passing by on their way to school in the morning, for instance.

The trucker looked dubious and ominously filled the space directly in front of the haystack, scouring for any trace of evidence. Fortunately for my brothers, the tracks between the haystack and the feeding area looked as if they belonged there. The trucker finally slammed back into his truck and drove off. As soon as we were sure it was safe, we gave the all clear, and our brothers emerged from the secret room. We had passed the initiation, whether we meant to or not. That morning we moved up a notch on the trustworthy scale and on the general male worthiness ladder.

THE DAY Stan claimed to be able to hypnotize a chicken is one I'll never forget.

"Chickens can't be hypnotized!" I protested.

Now, we weren't allowed to gamble or make bets, but of course we did. Often the wager was a dare with an inherent threat of failure or some other act of humiliation. In this case, Stan wagered a swift kick in the backside. What this meant was the loser would have to bend over, grab his ankles, and let the other boy kick as hard as he could. This also happened to be a form of discipline the older boys adopted to keep the younger ones in line, so I was quite familiar with it from personal experience. If they caught me doing something wrong, they would point out the infraction and threaten to tell one of the mothers—or I could bend over and take the punishment they meted out like a man.

Mark reasoned that Stan wouldn't make such a wager if he couldn't back it up, but I was caught up in the illogical nature of his claim. Plus, I fantasized about Stan having to bend over and grab his ankles while I gave him a swift kick.

"I'll take the bet," I declared. I stuck out my hand and we shook on it. I knew I was going to regret it the instant the grin cracked his face.

Stan knelt down on the ground in some soft loose dirt and used his thighs to hold the chicken between his legs. With his left hand, Stan grabbed the chicken around the neck close to the base of its skull, where he could control the movement of its head. Then he pinned the chicken's head to the ground with its beak in the dirt. With his free hand, he began drawing a straight line in the dirt from the tip of the chicken's beak, out about a foot. Then he drew another line but didn't touch the beak.

I was starting to sweat. Stan really looked like he knew what he was doing. He drew this line over and over, about fifty times, then slowly loosened his grip on the bird. Eventually, he had let go completely, but the chicken didn't move. It stayed right there gazing at the line even though Stan was no longer touching it. He stopped drawing the line and gently walked away from the chicken. I stared in amazement for about three or four minutes as the chicken didn't move, not even a twitch.

Finally a fly landed next to the line and broke the trance. The chicken quickly stood up and looked around, as if it were wondering how in the world it had ended up on the ground with its neck stretched out and its beak in the dirt.

"Time to pay up," Stan announced.

I couldn't do anything. It had been a fair bet, and the evidence was clearly displayed. This was going to hurt. I knew from experience that Stan's goal would be to kick so hard that I would topple headfirst onto the ground. I scanned the area to make sure it was clear of cow pies, thistles, or anthills—then bent over, grabbed my ankles, and waited for the worst. Looking between my legs, I spotted Stan off to the left setting up in much the same fashion as a field-goal kicker. I closed my eyes as he started his run toward me. His aim wasn't for the large, cushioned portion of my backside, but just underneath, hoping to create a trajectory and concurrent velocity to dramatically increase the probability I would do a header. I felt my feet lift off and knew he had achieved his objective.

Winded, I lay on the ground and looked at the sky. My backside throbbed. I felt like I'd been kicked by a mule—and at that moment thought a mule would have made a much better brother.

Having once again demonstrated his dominance, Stan was ready to move on. It wasn't much later that he was ready to teach Mark and me how to handle the roosters so we could take on the chore of feeding the chickens. The roosters really made me panic, and I dreaded opening the coop. My first attempt at rooster control was a disaster, and I was ready to give up.

"Get back down here," Stan demanded. "We aren't going to let you become a chicken for the rest of your life."

I hated the thought that my brothers would think I was a chicken. It was hard enough being at the bottom of the brother ladder without their thinking I was a chicken to boot. This was a reputation I was not willing to live with, so I assumed the position for my next lesson in handling the roosters and keeping them from attacking me when I entered the coop.

Stan kept saying things like, "I'm not gonna let you grow up to be a crybaby mama's boy, is that clear?"

I nodded. I didn't want to grow up to be a crybaby mama's boy, either. I wanted to be courageous like Stan, strong like Paul, fast like Steve. But most of all I wanted my brothers to respect me as one of them. I didn't want to be an outcast. It was bad enough that my father seemed to have no use for me; I couldn't stand it if my brothers were to feel that way as well.

Stan grabbed my face and turned it so my attention was on him, not the rooster. He tried to persuade me that my jeans and boots would protect me from any real damage the rooster would try to inflict, and all I had to do was step up and give him a swift kick. I thought about what Stan said and realized I was afraid of nothing but a chicken that I could stomp into the ground if I determined to. I wanted so badly for my older brothers to approve of me that I dug deep inside and conquered my rooster fears.

ONE DAY, I went out looking for the older four boys. I snuck out of the house thinking they were in the barn doing something they wanted to hide from Mark and me. But, to my surprise, they weren't there. Instead they were behind the cinderblock house. Stan had in his hands a BB gun—which is something I knew was strictly forbidden. He looked at me angrily and cocked the gun. Consumed by the fear that surged through me when he pointed the gun my way, I turned and ran. Stan was right behind me, though. He took aim as I galloped across the road. Just as my feet hit the grass of the front yard, I felt a sharp sting in my lower back and fell to the ground screaming. Steve and Paul came running. They carried me captive back behind the cinderblock house, out of view of anyone in the big house.

"What do you think you're doing?" Stan demanded, as Steve and Paul pulled up my shirt to look at where I'd been hit. The BB had wedged itself into the skin without fully breaking through. I was freaking out—crying and screaming and not doing a very good job of deflecting attention. Paul used his fingernail to scratch the BB out. After I stopped crying, Stan changed his tactic.

"Do you ever want to be included in anything we do?" he asked.

Of course I did!

"Or do you want to be blackballed forever?" Stan continued. "I'm sorry I shot you, but you took off and I had to stop you. If you tell them about the gun, they will take it away, and you will never get to fire it."

Okay, he had my attention now.

"And if they punish me, I'll make sure you get punished too. You'll be an outcast. You'll never be able to do anything with us again. I will make your life a living hell."

Well, I didn't like the sound of that, but I believed Stan. He let me think about it for a minute before sealing the deal.

"If you don't tell, I'll let you fire it and teach you how to shoot." He walked over to some empty soda cans and lined them up, then cocked the gun. "Come on, give it a try."

Stan held the gun out to me. Steve and Paul nodded in approval. A kid who craved approval as much as I did reveled in moments like this. I reached out and took the gun and listened carefully to Stan's instructions.

As I took aim and pulled the trigger, I knew I was now a willing accomplice in their crime. It was worth it because even more important I was being trusted with a secret, and if I proved faithful in keeping it, I would be trusted with other secret knowledge they'd kept hidden from me and the rest of the family.

We did a lot of dangerous things, just trying to prove to each other that we could, that we weren't afraid, that we could be the best, that we were growing into men worthy of being gods. The six of us spent protracted lengths of time together and enjoyed each other. However, the hierarchy was always there. Little did we know that one day we might be competing against each other for the privilege of staying in the community and receiving wives. Whether we knew it or not, we had to "get it right" in the way we established ourselves with each other as children, because one day we would go through the same process as men competing against other men in our community.

4

Public School

Wo unto the liar, for he shall be thrust down to hell.

—*Book of Mormon, 2 Nephi 9:34*

The move into the big house in Sandy was the first time since the raid of 1953 that Father felt safe enough from prosecution to be able to live permanently in relative peace with his wives and their children together in one house. However, it was an uneasy peace. At any moment authorities could come after people living the principle of plural marriage. Living together in one house under one name carried the risk of drawing more attention to our family, though, so my parents took measures to protect us that I didn't know about when I was young.

When I later joined the navy, I made a startling discovery. As you might expect, I had to produce my birth certificate. Imagine my surprise at learning that when I was born, I was given the last name of Chapman, not Mackert. Instead of carrying my father's name, I bore the maiden name of my father's mother. That was pretty convoluted! In order to conceal my father's identity, my birth certificate said I was the son of Clyde

Chapman, not Clyde Mackert. But that wasn't the half of it. At the time of my birth, Mom was uncertain if Father had made a final decision about my first name. She knew the last name would be Chapman, so she'd filled in that part of the form, and she thought my first name would be Brian, but she wasn't sure. In a moment of indecision, she stopped herself from writing in the name. She only went as far as the downstroke on the capital B. The hospital waited three days, and when Mom didn't get back to them in time, they filed the birth certificate with the name "1 Chapman." Yes, that was my legal name! It was bad enough being one of thirty-one siblings and feeling like a number. Now I found out that my birth certificate had actually confirmed it.

Many of my mother's children went through similar experiences. With the exception of Rena and David, all my siblings' birth certificates listed the father as Roy Mackert, though there was no such person. My parents had borrowed Uncle Roy Johnson's first name and added Father's last name to create a completely fictional character who had supposedly sired four of my siblings. Mom was pregnant with Rena during the raid of 1953, so there wasn't much point in hiding her father's identity; she is the only one whose birth certificate is truthful about who her father really was. David, who was the next one born after the raid, didn't even have a birth certificate to document his birth.

When I enrolled in public school, my parents amended my birth certificate, giving me a real first name and identifying my father accurately. Now it appeared as if my mother hadn't known who my father was when I was born and had to amend the document to the correct listed father's name. That certainly didn't do much to enhance my mother's image. It wasn't until I was older that I understood just how shady all of this lying to conceal Father's identity made my mother's reputation appear. According to government records, she was having multiple children by multiple men apart from my father, her husband who was not really her husband according to law, but another woman's husband—Mother Midge. Despite what it did to my mother's reputation, the lying and chronic deceit was justified because it protected Father and kept the principle of plural marriage alive. Anything was justifiable for the sake of building God's kingdom.

With all of us living under the same roof, the lies of the past wouldn't work. It would have been impossible to have that many children trying to keep their stories straight about their pretend relationships to each other in order to conceal the truth of their common paternity. Even with the same last name it wasn't easy, because some of us were so close in age that we couldn't possibly have had the same mother, but far enough apart in birth dates that we couldn't possibly be twins. Several times three mothers gave birth in the same year. One year, Howard, David, and Shem were all born within eleven days to three different mothers.

My birthday fell too late in the school year for me to start public school a year ahead of Mark, so even though he was younger by nine months, we started school together. With the same name and the same address, questions were sure to arise. I was instructed to tell people my birthday was September 9, the same as Mark's, and that we were twins. I was also told to call my mother "Aunt Myra" and address Mother Donna as "Mom" in public.

I remember the first time my mother came to pick us up from school. Upon seeing the old blue Dodge Dart pull up, I ran out to the car waving my arms and calling out, "Mom!" My mother was a quick thinker and responded, "Your mother isn't with me today. It's just me, but she's waiting for you at home." As soon as I was in the car and the door was shut, Mom immediately scolded me for calling her "Mom" in public. I can't imagine how this affected her, rebuking her own son for acknowledging she was his mother. I do know how it affected me. It felt as if my mother was somehow ashamed of me and didn't want me to be known as her child. I was a liability and had done nothing to deserve it. As an adult, I later understood the reasoning, but as a kindergartner, it hit me in the gut. This was all too complex for a six-year-old to comprehend and remember. And I also faced the terrifying knowledge that I had somehow let the cat out of the bag, and it would be my fault if the police raided our house in the middle of the night to arrest Father and cart us all off to foster care. It was a great weight for a child to bear.

I ATTENDED kindergarten and first grade at Hillcrest Elementary. I remember being presented with my very first set of brand-new clothes to wear on the first day of school. Everything from head to toe was new. Even better, there were two sets of clothes, not one! These clothes had never been worn by another living soul; I would be the first to don them. I took them and held them up to my face to breathe in deeply the blissful scent of something truly new. Until then, all of my clothes came to me second or third hand. My brother Ken was a few years older and always wore things before I did, and his clothes came down to either Mark or me with fresh patches over the old ones. Occasionally clothes that were "new" to me had been purchased in a secondhand store and were several seasons out of style. By the time bell-bottoms made it into my wardrobe, they had come and gone in the rest of the world.

But these clothes were brand new!

After Mom presented me with my new school clothes, she told me to take them to Father's study and put a slip of paper on them with my name on it. I knew those clothes were meant for me. Mom had procured them especially for me, but I had to wait for Father to give them to me—which meant I had to deserve them. They wouldn't just be a free gift to a little boy excited and nervous about starting school. The clothes had to be a life lesson dispensed by my controlling father. He wanted us to understand where our blessings came from, and the right answer wasn't from God, but from Father. He would determine if we had been good enough to deserve whatever item one of the mothers in the household wanted to present to a child. Sometimes things would sit in his study for weeks on end. We would peer inside to see if an item meant for one of us was still there with the same name attached to it. As long as it was, there was still hope that one day we would deserve to receive it. In the meantime we would scurry around trying to please Father in every little thing and hasten the day we would deserve his blessing.

Years later, as an adult, I discovered that Father's need to control included even feminine hygiene products for my sisters. Father had occasionally withheld them from my sister Rena because he didn't think she had been worthy even of this essential item. Rena was forced to use the old-time method of protecting her clothes during her period by using rags. I cannot imagine the impact this must have had on the self-esteem of a teenage girl! How could her father think she was so dirty and unworthy as a woman that she was not deserving of feminine hygiene?

When Father called us to his study to receive an item, generally a lecture was part of the package. If we had committed an offense and he wanted to make a point of it, he would announce that anyone who had anything in the study should meet him there after morning prayers. He would hand out all the items to those he found worthy and save the item for the offending child for last. If you were the last one standing there, you were sure to suffer a reprimand and be sent away empty-handed. Everyone else would know you had been sent away.

In the case of my new school clothes, I knew that school would start in only two more days, and Father still hadn't called me into the study. With dismay, I imagined having to wear old clothes to the first day of school—tormented by the knowledge that brand-new clothes were just out of reach behind a closed door. When Father finally called for me, my heart pounded in my throat as I entered the study. I nodded numbly as Father strictly charged me not to wear the clothes anywhere except to school. When I got home, I was supposed to change immediately into my regular clothes more suited for farm chores. I carried my new clothes down to the room I shared with Mark and laid them on my bed. Holding them up over and over again, I agonized over which combination of shirt and pants I should wear on the first day. I had two pairs of pants, two long sleeve shirts, a new belt, and new tennis shoes. After hours of internal debate, I finally made a selection and put the other set away.

EVEN WITH my new clothes, it wasn't going to be hard to tell that something was different about me. No one else wore long sleeves, rolled down, when the weather was still this warm. No one wore every button secured up to the neck. "Normal" kids wore short sleeves at that time of year, with buttons open at the collar. But I would have been considered an apostate if I dared to be that comfortable. Loosening my collar would have been a sure sign that I was falling away from the true faith, and even as a six-year-old, I understood that I should never toy with my eternal salvation.

The dress code was just as bad for girls. They were only allowed to wear dresses, and the hem could be no higher than mid-calf, preferably falling between the ankle and mid-calf. Sleeves had to be full length, and the neckline couldn't come down below the collarbone. If a blouse had buttons, every button had to be fastened. The rule of thumb was that the only parts of your body that could show flesh were your hands, feet, head, and neck; anything below the collarbone was not allowed. If a girl was caught with a button undone or a sleeve rolled up when she was not in the act of washing dishes or doing some chore that required protecting her clothing, she was deemed a hussy. This was a double standard because boys were allowed to test the boundaries and relax the rules a little bit when out of the public eye, but for girls there was no grace even on the warmest days in private settings.

In kindergarten, Mark and I were the biggest children in the class, with the exception of Bobby. He was about half a head taller than us and a bit heavier. All the kids in our class wanted Mark and me to fight Bobby simply because we were the three biggest kids in the class and they wanted to see what would happen. Mark and I liked Bobby and didn't have any bones to pick with him that would warrant a fight, so we always refused our classmates' attempts to instigate a scuffle. We thought we were fitting in just fine at the beginning of our public school careers.

In first grade, that all changed. As we walked to school other kids called us "polygs" or "polyg kids." They meant it as an insult, but it became a badge of honor within our community. The term "Mormon" originally was intended as derogatory as well. I can almost hear the disdain hissing through the teeth as early enemies of the Church called my third and fourth great-grandfathers "Mormons." The term evolved to bringing pride to those who bore it. "Polyg" had undergone the same metamorphosis. But it was not Gentiles deriding us; it was mainstream Mormons. We experienced the same persecutions our forefathers experienced, for the same beliefs they stood for, from the very people who knew the truth and abandoned it.

I remember once a group of high school students in a pickup pulled a U-turn in front of us as we walked along. They started throwing rocks at us as they sped away hollering, "Polygs!" Mark and I dodged the rocks in a surge of adrenaline, but the incident stung. After that, the other first graders figured out we were "polygs" and didn't want anything to do with us, treating us with the same disdain they'd seen in the older kids. The only real friends Mark and I had were each other.

One time, I hid outside after the recess bell had rung signaling it was time for my class to go in. I wanted to see if anyone would even notice I was missing. Used to fading into the background of a large household at home, I wondered if it was any different at school. If someone noticed my absence, it might mean someone cared, and a seven-year-old boy needs someone to care. Well trained at home in having a story ready for every occasion, I had it all figured out that, if discovered, I would claim I was out at the end of the baseball field and didn't hear the bell.

I hid in a ditch where the grass was tall because the mower couldn't maneuver that depth. From a distance, I watched as my teacher carefully scanned the recess yard for stragglers and then took the class inside. Shortly after she disappeared into the building, the older grades let out for their recess. With dozens of children engaged in play activities, I couldn't resist and came out of hiding to join them.

At the monkey bars I watched older boys competing to see who could make it across the bars and turn around and come back while skipping every other bar as they swung through the air. Used to having to prove myself to older siblings, I climbed up the opposite end of the structure to see if I could perform this amazing feat. The boy at the far end was about the age of my brother Ken, four years older than I, and he smiled broadly when he noticed me. That should have been my first clue, but I was only in first grade.

"Do you know how to play 'Chicken'?" he asked with a smirk on his face.

I had played this game with kids my own age and it seemed innocent enough. In "Chicken," two opponents would swing out to the middle of the monkey bars and joust with their legs until one of them managed to pull the other off the bar.

"Sure, I know how to play," I answered confidently.

"Ya wanna play now?" he asked.

I looked around. Everyone on the playground was bigger and stronger than I was. Even in my naïveté, the sudden burning in my stomach told me this was not going to be a fair match. But there was no backing down now. That wasn't the polyg way. I accepted his challenge by swinging out into the middle of the monkey bars. He followed suit. I had the good fortune of arriving at the middle of the bars before he did, but I made the fatal error of stopping and losing the momentum of my swing. My opponent came upon me with his full swing, raising his legs up to clamp around me like a vice. He yanked me from the bar in the blink of an eye. I landed flat on my back on the sand, the wind knocked out of me. Gasping for air, I arched my back, trying not to cry. My opponent dropped easily from the bar and landed with his feet straddling me. He put his face down close to mine and laughed.

"What's the matter? Can't breathe?" Clearly he was gloating.

A blur flashed above me moving left to right, and suddenly he was gone. Dazed and trying to regain my senses along with my breath, I sat up to see what had become of my antagonist. All I saw was a cloud of dust in the middle of a clump of cheering kids. I could hear their voices urging, "Come on! Kick that polyg's butt!"

What polyg? The older boy had already proven himself against me. So where was he?

I pushed through the crowd and discovered what had become of my antagonist. He was lying on his back desperately trying to block the volley of punches unleashed upon him by another older boy who sat on his belly and pummeled him. The other kid was merciless! He just kept the punches coming and knew right where he wanted to land them.

It was my brother Ken! He had come at my opponent with a flying tackle and almost knocked the boy out of his shoes. The bully was now crying and begging Ken to stop. Ken would pause long enough for the boy to think he was finished, then he'd let loose another round.

"You like picking on little kids, do you?" Ken taunted between punches. "Makes you feel really tough, doesn't it?" More punches. "Next time you're feeling all big and bad, come and try me instead. Then you'll find out whether you're a man!"

A teacher finally broke through the crowd and pulled Ken to his feet. I knew Ken was in trouble, and it was entirely my fault for being out after recess. He looked at me as they took him into the building and eventually to the principal's office. The look he gave me filled me with pride. It said, "We're family, and I've got your back."

Ken and I had always had a strange relationship. We fought a lot, and I couldn't understand why. I always assumed he just didn't like me. I was too young to understand the reasons, and wouldn't for many years to come. But there he was, fighting my fight against a foe bigger and older than I. Sure, we'd fought among ourselves. But when push came to shove, we took care of each other. That day Ken proved to me that he really loved me in spite of all the fighting we did with each other. Deep down he cared enough to feel responsible for my safety and well-being.

This was one of the first experiences that taught me the code of honor among my brothers. You never fight an unfair fight, and there is no honor in beating a disadvantaged opponent. You are a coward if you pull a knife, a bat, or any other weapon. You never gang up on an opponent, and you certainly never pick a fight with someone younger than you. If you get into a fair fight with someone, my brothers will let you lose rather than jumping in to save you. If you lose, it means you either need to learn to fight better or have the wisdom not to pick a fight with someone stronger than you. God help me if I ever lost a fair fight, because it meant every one of my older brothers was going to take me home, put on the boxing gloves and teach me everything he knew about fighting. Father had been a boxer in college, and we all sought his approval by trying to be the best.

At Hillcrest Elementary I met my first black person. In the FLDS we only used the term "Negro." Although the wider culture was changing and the word had fallen out of use in favor of "black" or "African American," we stuck to our language. American culture during civil rights years pressed for equality between the races, but we knew this was not God's way. Our leaders railed against mingling with the seed of Cain, which was Satan's attempt to snuff out the authority of the priesthood on earth. Negroes could never hold the Mormon priesthood in this lifetime, and marrying someone of the seed of Cain meant spiritual death.

The boy I met at Hillcrest was in the same grade as Ken, Laura, and Camille. At the time, I didn't fully understand the reasons for the prejudice we felt against him; I just knew we were supposed to feel it. Unfortunately, this boy didn't know anything about Mormons and made the mistake of publicizing that he had a crush on my sister Laura. One day all the kids were chasing each other in a game of tag. I came around the corner of the school to see Ken slam this child up against the wall, all the while cussing furiously and raising his hand as if he were preparing to strike. I wondered what had happened because Ken didn't generally go off like that without a reason. Later I found out the boy had been chasing Laura, and when he caught her, he tried to kiss her. Ken was fulfilling his duties as our family code dictated. He was protecting Laura from the unwanted sexual advance of a man—and not just any man, but a member of the cursed race of Cain.

With experiences like that, I quickly became aware of just how different we were and that we didn't really fit in at all. Ignorance had been bliss; now it was all destroyed. First grade turned out to be my last year in public school. Father had become increasingly concerned with the things the public school was teaching. Between evolution, sex education, school prayer, the wearing of shorts or T-shirts in gym, and other controversial topics, Father had had enough. He withdrew all his children from the public school system. But we had no clue during that summer. Father didn't inform us of his decision until the time came to prepare for the next school year. That's when we learned we wouldn't be going back to school; instead, Mother Donna would teach us at home.

Our withdrawal accomplished another objective: It took us out of the public eye. Father's authority would go unchallenged by the erroneous ideas of Gentiles. And within the confines of our own property, it would be much easier to keep our family secrets.

The year I started school was the year the tenuous balance of power in the Priesthood Council began to unravel. Carl Holm, one of the Apostles, died in 1972. As president of the council and Prophet of the FLDS, Uncle Roy should have replaced Carl Holm with another Apostle, but he didn't. Uncle Roy advocated the one-man doctrine, and appointing another Apostle would have undermined his own position that he didn't particularly need the counsel of another man to discern revelations from God. In withdrawing us from public school, my father pulled his children closer to the FLDS core at the same time that the core began its trajectory toward the explosion of power that became Warren Jeffs.

5

Polyg Elementary

And that wicked one (Satan) cometh and taketh away
light and truth, through disobedience, from the children
of men, and because of the tradition of their fathers.

—*Doctrine and Covenants, Section 93:39*

It didn't take long for word to spread in our polygamist community that Father was teaching his children at home, and other families soon wanted in on the action. Other than the public school, the only alternative was the school run by Apostle Rulon Jeffs called Alta View Academy. Jeffs didn't have much more room to expand his school, so the possibility of another private school sparked a lot of interest.

Before the 1953 raid on Short Creek, Father had been principal of the local school there. Because he considered himself "experienced in education," this is one of the factors that made him decide his younger children should be homeschooled in Sandy twenty years later. Under Father's supervision, Mother Donna took the helm as our new school principal and teacher. In the first year, our little "Mountain View

Academy" had seven students in grades one through eight. In the course of seven years of existence, the school grew to around 250 students. After eighth grade, students had the option of finishing high school through the public school system or through correspondence courses. Father made arrangements with a school in Chicago for correspondence. Parents could choose the path for their children or simply end their education after eighth grade, which was quite common.

In the first year of Mountain View Academy, we had one other polyg kid from outside our family. His name was Ian, and he was the same age as Mark and me. It was nice to have a classmate who was not part of our family. The school began in our basement, in the recreation room near the girls' end. As other families started enrolling their children, Father charged a fee that covered the cost of materials. He bought old used textbooks from the public school system—along with desks, chairs, and other supplies—at their annual surplus sale. And rather than competing, Father's school and Rulon Jeffs's school helped each other take care of the children of the community.

While all of this was happening, more of Father's children were reaching marriageable age—mid-teens for the girls—and being paired off by the Priesthood Council. As the family's need for bedrooms decreased, the school's need for space increased. The recreation rooms in our basement could no longer contain the number of children coming to our school. Father decided to move the remaining girls out of the basement and put them in the upstairs nursery rooms that were not being used, since all of Father's wives were beyond childbearing years by then. Father organized us into work crews, and we ripped out the walls of the girls' end of the basement and sectioned off three classrooms. We also used the small cinderblock house across the road as a classroom, so we had a total of four rooms, with two grades in each room. Every year was a juggling act to make the most of the limited space we had.

When the remodeling project began, all of us boys armed ourselves with hammers, crowbars, or anything else we could use to break through the sheetrock. We started in the girls' recreation room and lined up in the spaces between the two-by-four studs in the wall. Once the signal was given, we all raced to the last room in the girls' end, and on the way we smashed and clawed our way through the sheetrock, stepping over studs as we advanced. It was great fun to be so destructive and have the full permission of our parents to tear the house apart, literally. With all the boys flailing about with hammers, it was amazing no one was seriously hurt. After all the sheetrock was torn from the walls and carried out, we left the weight-bearing walls and destroyed everything else we didn't need in the new floor plan. After gutting the girls' end, we put up new walls, created bathrooms for boys and girls, and prepared for the first day of school.

Father also paved what was supposed to be a tennis court and basketball court to the east of the big house. This slab ended up being used as the place for parents to pull in and drop off their children in the morning and pick them up in the afternoons. Cars would stop where the sidewalk led from the backside of the house to the school's entrance into the basement. We installed a privacy fence to shield children from public view as they were dropped off or picked up.

Parents had plenty of opportunity to become involved in their children's education. Father enlisted parents to volunteer their time assisting in teaching at the school and offered families a waiver on the modest tuition for doing so. Some of my older siblings became teachers to help the effort of the school—Karen, Steve, and Laura were all teachers at one time or another.

In the afternoon when school let out, Ken, Mark, and I found ourselves saddled with regular janitorial chores. We were responsible for cleaning the classrooms and the restrooms and making sure everything was ready for the next day. Taking care of the janitorial duties was no small task, especially after enrollment swelled. Every day, three elementary-age boys cleaned four rooms big enough to hold an average of fifty or more students each, and the restrooms to support that student population. And, of course, this work did not get us off the hook of the regular chores around the farm.

Mountain View Academy had a board of trustees to provide oversight and to govern the operations of the school. In reality, though, the trustees did very little; Mother Donna took care of the operational needs of the school without involving them. However, one of the duties of the trustees was to deal with students who proved to have the most serious disciplinary problems—like me! Father was the head of the board, naturally, and therefore held the highest level of authority for the school. A child who was unruly, disobedient, or disrespectful of those in authority was suspended until a meeting could be arranged between child, parents, and the trustees. The general rule was that a child who was suspended three times was also expelled. The reason I know the "three strikes and you're out" rule so well is that I was suspended—and expelled—from the school more times than any other student.

Mother Donna and I had a love-hate relationship at times. She was a strict disciplinarian, and I resented her for it because it seemed to me that the lion's share of her skill was expended solely on my discipline. I also came to understand that I had the ability to push her buttons. In a public setting like a classroom where she was both principal and teacher, different rules applied than did in our home life. For example, Father once had to let a teacher go because she popped a kid in class, so I knew where the line was on this issue. I could act out in class and get on Mother Donna's nerves all I wanted, and she couldn't hit me. To me, this was real power—or at least the first real power I had experienced. I would utter things I thought were witty, yet bordering on disrespectful. I would shoot spit wads and rubber bands at classmates, or pass notes just to see how much I could get away with before the hammer came down. Mark, Mother Donna's own son, was one of my favorite comrades in mischief, but somehow he almost always escaped her notice and I consistently got caught. Mother Donna knew better than to strike me in front of others or during school hours and reserved punishment for after school. It didn't take me long to figure out that often she was just too tired or preoccupied by then to deal with me, and I would get away with my antics for the day. But not always. Sometimes I had to pay the price.

I lost count of how many times I was expelled from Father's school. Each time, I was reinstated simply because there wasn't much option. Father wasn't about to send me back to public school, and it was too much of a bother to send me to Alta View Academy. Can you imagine my father, a school official and head of a polygamous household, trying to explain to the Apostle Rulon Jeffs why he wanted his son to attend Alta View? He wasn't about to admit that he couldn't control his own unruly son. The only solution was to suspend me for a period of time, let me suffer from boredom upstairs, and then when they felt I had learned my lesson for the time being, readmit me to the school.

While I was on suspension, I watched other kids go outside to play in the yard during recess. I wasn't allowed outside; letting me have a little fun would contradict the purpose of my suspension. So one view that became familiar to my classmates was my face in the window as I twisted and contorted my features to amuse them. I did whatever I could to gain their attention. Mother Donna would predictably send an older sibling to check up on me and make sure I wasn't misbehaving during school hours. I also had additional chores as a form of punishment during these suspensions. In the end, I was desperate to return to class and willing to say or do anything to be readmitted. I only met with the full board of trustees one time, and that was early on in my long rap sheet. As my suspensions became more of a regular occurrence, occasionally I had to see Father to be reinstated, but generally he left it to Mother Donna as the principal of the school to reinstate me. If I'd been anyone else's kid, I'd have been a goner. But then, if I'd been anyone else's kid, I wouldn't have found pushing Mother Donna's buttons so much fun and wouldn't have been in so much trouble.

In all fairness to Mother Donna, my real resentment toward her wasn't because I felt unfairly treated. Looking back, I feel I resented her simply because she wasn't my mom. My own mother worked all day and often came home long after I was already in bed. I know now she was using her job to hide from the pain in her marriage. Mom worked in a cancer clinic, and the married doctor she worked for was in love with her and wanted Mom to run away with him. Mom cared for him, but not to the point where she would leave her husband. For her the contrast between home and work was dramatic. At work she was with a man who adored her and didn't want to share her with anyone. He was even willing to forsake his own family for her. At home, though, Mom was just another wife helping a man to become a god and had to share her husband's affections with three other women. At home was nothing but a loneliness even her children could not comfort.

Mom was also beaten down in her role as a mother. In plural marriages, it's not unusual for one wife to emerge as dominant, and in our house that was Mother Donna. The other wives accused Mom of being overprotective of her children and unable to discipline them. When Mom was around, she tried to make up for her absence by spoiling me. When she did have time and energy to spend with me, she preferred to be doing enjoyable activities rather than punishing me. Knowing this, I played the part of the sweet, innocent, misunderstood, picked-on, and orphaned child around her. Because she worked long hours and didn't want to discipline us when she was home, she was pressured into abandoning her role as our mother.

Mother Midge was gentle and not a strict disciplinarian, though she knew how to put us on a guilt trip. But she also worked, so any free time she had was taken up with her relationships with her own children. Mother Maurine had not really bought into the plural marriage hierarchy. She looked after her own children and behaved the way she wanted to, leading the other wives to regard her as a wanton woman. She didn't involve herself much with the rest of us.

By default, Mother Donna became the primary mother figure in my life. In all honesty, I needed Mother Donna's discipline, but at the time I resented it because a boy needs his own mother. So when I was punished by Mother Donna for a sibling's offense, I saw it as prejudice on her part. Something closer to the truth is that Mother Donna was human and couldn't see everything or right every wrong. I know that now.

MARK AND I would often put on the gloves for a boxing match, and usually this ended in a draw. I would win one round, Mark would win the next. We were perfectly matched in speed, agility, and body structure. We had the same reach, the same height, the same weight. Only one person ever saw the two of us go toe-to-toe without the gloves—trying our best to kill each other. That person was Ken. Looking back on it now,

Mark and I should have beaten the tar out of Ken rather than each other because Ken had instigated the whole thing.

The three of us were going about our daily chores cleaning the school. All that was left was to vacuum. We had a canister vacuum that wasn't particularly easy to maneuver around the classroom furniture. It worked best if one person worked the hose and head, and another followed to be sure the canister didn't get caught on the legs of desks; so sometimes we did it that way rather that delegating the chore to one person. On this day, Ken decided to pull rank as the older brother and act bossy. He told Mark and me that he didn't care who did what as long as someone did the work.

Mark spoke up and said he would do the vacuuming and I should follow with the caboose. Normally, I wouldn't have made an issue of it, but for some reason that day I wasn't in the mood for being bossed around by my younger—by nine whole months—brother. My father had twelve biological sons, and Mark was the only one younger than I was—the only one below me in the family hierarchy. Who was he to tell me what job I would do?

"I'm older," I said indignantly, "so we'll do it my way. I'll vacuum and you follow."

"Are you going to take that?" Ken taunted Mark.

Mark looked at Ken, then looked at me and said, "Who died and made you king? I said I would vacuum and you push the caboose."

Ken was playing both sides of the fence. Just in case I had suddenly lost my bearings about the authority structure of the house, he reminded me. "Brian, you're older. He's supposed to obey you."

I pushed Mark to assert my dominance. "I said I'm vacuuming."

"Over my dead body," Mark said, pushing me back.

That was all it took. It was on. Mark and I began swinging in a furious exchange of blows while Ken sat back and enjoyed the spectacle he had created. At first, neither Mark nor I gained any ground. Then things started getting out of hand. As we tumbled around the classroom, we knocked over desks and chairs, trash cans and bookcases. We fought our way out into the hall and then into the next classroom. Mark would gain the advantage, then I would rally and strip it from him. Ken followed closely, sometimes trying to rescue the furniture without having to put a stop to the fight.

Mark and I worked our way through every part of the school. We even went in a bathroom, where we crashed through a stall partition, ripping it from its brackets. Finally, Mark gave me a quick uppercut that sent my head back into the wall, and as my head bounced, he landed a punch to my left eye and pinned my head to the wall. It felt as if my eyeball had been forced to the back of my skull. I slid down the wall and sat on the floor, holding my eye. I was too tired to fight anymore, and too concerned about my vision—which was missing in action at the moment. Suddenly Mark was not worried about winning, but about whether I was all right.

Ken roared with delighted laughter and applauded the courageous brawl. He was so pleased with himself that he told us he would vacuum by himself as long as no one heard about this. As my vision began to resurface, we surveyed the damage. In one classroom a whole line of desks had toppled like dominoes. My vision was still blurry, but I joined my brothers in straightening up the mess. The damage done to the walls and bathroom stalls we would simply report as things we'd noticed that needed to be repaired.

Despite Ken's cautions not to spread the news, he couldn't contain himself. He told Stan, Steve, and Paul when they arrived home from their jobs at Rulon Jeffs's jewelry shop. There was no shame in losing a fight fought well. Ken knew it, Mark knew it, and I knew it. Later Mark confessed to me that he was thankful he had landed what he called a lucky blow, because he was afraid it easily could have been him at the other end of a fortuitous punch. We agreed we never wanted to fight again without the gloves on.

It wasn't until I was in the fifth or sixth grade that I began to take much notice of girls. Mark and I would poke fun at each other by pairing the other with the ugliest girls so we could tease each other about fictitious crushes. Several girls in our school were good lookers, though. Amazingly, the majority of them were Barlow girls. But then again, the majority of the girls who attended our school were Barlow girls. I hated to admit they were pretty, because Barlow kids had such a swelled head about their lineage. John Y. Barlow started the FLDS with Uncle Roy S. Johnson. The Barlow men considered themselves to be the crème de le crème of the fundamentalist polygamist Mormons. Most of the rest of us considered the Barlows to be stuck up. But boy were their daughters something to look at, especially when you're eleven or twelve!

I supposed it was hopeless to think that one day any of these good-looking Barlow girls might marry me. You had to be the son of someone important to marry a good-looking girl—either that, or her first cousin. Many of the Barlow girls I went to school with ended up marrying their first cousins. Surprisingly, both they and their parents weren't ignorant of the increased possibility of birth defects in the children of these unions, yet they married anyway. The only reasoning I could come up with for such couplings is that they believed God would bless the union and keep them from the hazards inherent in marrying a close relative. For them, there could be nothing grander than for one Barlow to marry another and keep it all in the family.

Some of these unions were first marriages, meaning the husband didn't have any other wives yet. Usually in these situations, the couple went through a legal marriage performed with a marriage license, blood tests, and the whole works. I asked one girl how her sister explained to the officials at city hall how she was related to the groom, who was also her first cousin. She said, "That's easy. They didn't tell them they were first cousins. Instead they said they were distant cousins and explained the relationship through a route in the family tree that showed they were related but not closely enough to prohibit marriage." I almost fell out of my chair!

One morning Mark and I were out shoveling snow while the school kids were arriving. Dorothy Barlow, one of our school's teachers, arrived early in her Chevy Suburban (we used to call them Mormon troop transports). Dorothy had a daughter named Marianne, who was stunning in the most pleasing of ways. All the boys wanted Marianne, and I was no exception. Mark and I used to argue about who was better suited for her. When Marianne rounded the corner of our house on her way to the cinderblock house that day, my heart leaped. I was enraptured! She was accompanied by her brother John, her sister Kathleen, and her cousins Carla and Colleen. John came running up to Mark and me as we leaned on our shovels gaping at the parade of the finest looking polyg girls we'd ever seen. John knew how enamored we were and knocked the shovel handles out from under us. The sudden loss of balance jarred us out of our trance.

"What's up?" John inquired.

"Nothing, man. Just trying to get the walks shoveled," Mark said, as we returned to work.

"Want to give us a hand?" I asked.

"Sure!" John reached for an extra shovel nearby.

Meanwhile, Marianne and the other girls were passing by. They fired off their usual witty barbs, which they deigned to bestow on mere mortals like Mark and me as they paraded around like goddesses. Marianne was very good at this banter and had just delivered a stinging blow. I don't remember what she said; I only remember what I did.

"Careful, or I'll bean you upside the head with a snowball," I threatened.

Marianne turned, winked at me, and said, "You wouldn't dare." She tossed her hair flirtatiously.

Both Mark and John started in on me. "You're not going to let her get away with that, are you?"

"Watch this," I said, as I started packing a snowball.

Marianne turned and saw that I was arming myself. Being the cool customer she was, she merely walked away as if she wasn't concerned in the least. She was about thirty yards away by now and felt safe, apparently. I continued to pack my snowball, hardening it with each compression. Then I moved sideways like a quarterback stepping out of the pocket and let it rip. I threw the snowball as high and hard as I could. I knew it would take everything I could give it to close the distance between Marianne and me.

Before the snowball had even reached the peak of its trajectory, we began to laugh; we could tell this was a well-aimed shot. As the snowball descended, we all made a high-pitched sound effect, like the scream a bomb makes just before impact. All three of us shouted, "Boom!" as the snowball exploded over the back of Marianne's head, then we fell to the ground laughing hysterically.

Marianne was furious and stomped off into the cinderblock house to rearrange her hair.

I suddenly realized how stupid I had been. Who in his right mind would bean the girl he had a crush on? If I'd had any fantasy about some-day marrying Marianne Barlow, I had just ruined it for all time.

I was guilt-ridden. The only thing to do was apologize. I had to finish clearing the walks first, but I hurried inside the cinderblock house as soon as I could. Unfortunately, by then, the rest of the class had heard all about my well-aimed snowball.

Marianne wouldn't even look at me.

I walked over to her desk and stood in front of it.

"Are you all right?" I asked.

"Yes," she answered, sounding carefree.

"Look, I'm sorry. I was just trying to scare you. I didn't think I'd hit you. Can you forgive me?"

"No big deal," she said. "Don't worry about it."

Marianne was always a good sport, even if she was a snobby Barlow.

WHEN THE school first opened, Ian, Mark, and I were inseparable. When the school began to grow, Ian became more and more distant from Mark and me. Ian's mother was a Barlow, and Ian adopted the same aloof attitude of his kinsmen. A big lad, Ian towered over Mark and me, and he probably outweighed us by twenty or thirty pounds. It seemed that every other day someone in the Barlow clan would persuade Ian to fight either Mark or me, and every other day Ian got the worst of it. Yes, Ian was a big kid, but his size hindered him when it came to speed and agility. Thanks to the many hours of training in boxing under the tutelage of our older brothers, Mark and I rarely came out on the losing end of a confrontation. We'd been in many fights with others our age as we tried to live up to the expectations of our older brothers and prove our manliness.

Dane Barlow, Ian's cousin, once played the part of the instigator in a dispute that erupted between Ian and me while the teachers had left the room for one reason or another. Ian had managed to get on my last nerve, and somehow I found myself with my back to the girls' bathroom. Dane yelled out to Ian, "Push him into the girls' bathroom!"

I saw the look on Ian's face and could tell the idea met with his approval. So I raised my hands and took a boxer's fighting stance to let him know it simply was not going to happen. Ian did not seem to register the threat. Instead, he stepped forward with arms raised, ready to push me into the girls' bathroom. I quickly assessed the situation and concluded this had just escalated into a physical confrontation, so I fired a warning shot to his chin to remind him who he was messing with.

Ian's face turned red with rage as he grabbed my left arm and held it down to create an opening through which he could land a punch with his right. I stood and waited for it—and ducked to the right as it glanced off my shoulder. I came up at him with an uppercut that made him let go of my arm. With both hands free, I unleashed an unrelenting volley. Having my back to the wall was not a position I was eager to prolong, and I was not about to let him embarrass me in front of the whole class.

One minute I was working Ian over, and the next I was punching air. I looked around. He was gone.

"Where did he go?" I asked Mark.

"He ran to the boys' bathroom," Mark informed me. "You should have seen it! As he was turning to run, you caught him right in the eye with an uppercut."

I stormed around the corner to the boys' bathroom and shoved the door open. Ian was standing in front of the sink with water running, holding his eye and looking in the mirror.

"Are you all right?" I asked.

"Yeah, but my eye is going to blacken."

"Sorry, man," I said, "but you shouldn't have tried to push me into the girls' bathroom. You didn't give me a choice."

"Don't worry about it," he said.

For a moment, I thought perhaps Ian and I could be friends again, like we had been the first years of the school. But fate wouldn't have it.

Against all odds, Dane Barlow declared Ian the victor in our confrontation. How can you claim someone is the victor when he turned and ran from the fight? I was the one still standing my ground. But the rest of the Barlows backed Dane and reminded us all who was important and who was not. Ian, in order to save face with his relatives, accepted their proclamation of victory by simply smiling when they made it. He looked at me from across the room with his eye red and swollen. I knew Ian was lost to me once and for all.

I was expelled for fighting, of course. Ian's mother had been childhood friends with both Mom and Mother Donna. The principal was faced with the horrifying embarrassment of her sister's son blackening the eye of their mutual friend's son. What could she possibly do? Ian had the black eye, and I was unscathed, so obviously that made me the aggressor. Mother Donna didn't even allow me to plead my case. Looking back, that injustice didn't matter. The rules said if you fought, you were expelled.

Only Ian wasn't expelled. I was.

Ian's mother was a Barlow. Mine was nothing in comparison. I was nothing but the youngest child of a third wife. The Barlows were at the top of the community hierarchy, and the Mackerts were somewhere in the bottom half. How many times was I going to have to learn that lesson? How many times was I going to have to learn the hard way that hierarchy of authority ruled my life, even in the classroom?

How long was I going to have to yearn to matter to somebody … anybody?

6

Something of My Own

Abraham received promises concerning his seed, and of the fruit of his loins … both in the world and out of the world should they continue as innumerable as the stars.

—Doctrine and Covenants, Section 132:30

It was a dream come true. We couldn't believe our good luck—getting a horse for free!

Father had rented out the field around our house in Sandy to a rancher looking for a place to graze his horses for the summer. Many of the mares had colts, and we boys reveled in watching the lot of them. One in particular, though, looked malnourished, and before long we realized he was a reject. His mother didn't even want him around, and none of the rest of the herd did, either. The rancher simply said he didn't expect the colt to survive, and that was just the way it was in nature. One colt just didn't matter all that much. It was hard not to feel sorry for the colt, and I recognized my own sense of rejection in what was happening to him.

But the colt, a dark brown Arabian with a black mane and tail, did survive. At the end of the summer, the rancher was amazed the colt was still alive and asked if we wanted it. Believe me, he didn't have to ask twice.

But then there was the small matter of convincing Father to let us keep a horse.

Immediately, all the boys jumped into making a list of reasons why we needed a horse on the farm: He could help with retrieving the cattle when they broke out of the pasture, he could help keep the neighbor's bull out of our pasture when our cows were in heat—and it would be safer to chase out the bull on horseback than on foot. The list went on and on, until we were ready to try it out on our mothers. We convinced each of them of the worthiness of our cause, and by the time Father arrived home from work, the family stood as a united front. He could either agree to let us keep the horse, or forever be the villain who denied his children a free horse that would more than earn its keep—which we were well aware was a distinct possibility if Father felt he had a point to prove. However, he gave us his nod; that was all we needed.

We set out to fatten up the horse, but even before that, we had to clean him up. Combing out his mane and tail proved fruitless; it was simpler just to cut the burs and tangles out, so we gave the colt a proper butch haircut—and the name stuck. We called him Butch.

The older boys didn't waste much time before putting a bit in his mouth and coaxing him to accept a bridle. My brother Paul taught me how to grab Butch by the nose so my hand pinched off the nostrils while shoving the bit against his teeth. The boys eventually triumphed and Butch was broken, and we could start riding him bareback. Butch caught on well to cutting cattle, and while we were glad to have him around for our own entertainment, he was very much a working animal. All you had to do was give him free rein and hang on tight, and Butch would corral the cattle like it was a job he was born to do.

AT A secondhand store, I saw a book on how to train horses to jump. I begged for it, and Mom bought it. Mark and I set out to teach Butch how to jump a rail, just like the horses in the steeple chases. The older boys were going to have nothing to do with this; we were going to do the job ourselves, and weren't they going to be impressed with the results! Ken thought we were crazy, and we were determined to prove him wrong.

Following the illustrations in the book, we first got Butch used to walking over a rail lying on the ground. We laid the two-by-four on the ground and led Butch over it. He fought us at first, but eventually he crossed the board. The book illustrated how to keep gradually setting the rail higher until the horse can no longer step over it, but has to jump. Butch did not like the looks of things when we raised the board to six inches off the ground, but Mark and I were not about to give up. Our reputation with our brothers was at stake by this time. They all knew what we were trying to do, and if we gave up now, we'd never hear the end of it. We persisted until Butch was capable of clearing a four-foot, eight-inch-high board.

The brothers were appropriately amazed. Mark and I had proven we could do it without their help and achieved a major milestone in our standing with the family.

I was always mesmerized by the animal stunts, especially the trick horseback-riding act at the circus. After we had Butch, I decided I could do that! I set out to learn how to ride a horse while standing up. One morning I rushed through my chores at lightning speed and spent the rest of the day trying to keep my balance while standing on Butch's back. By evening, I had triumphed.

Mom came home from work before dinner that day. I saw her car coming and raced her on Butch's back as she drove down our road. Mom went in the house to help with preparing dinner, and I led Butch through the pasture gate and rode him across the front of the house. I jumped up and stood as tall as I could and rode past the kitchen window, waving to those inside. At first I didn't catch anyone's attention, so I made another pass. This time Mom saw me. I waved at her, then turned and rode the horse across the yard.

"Brian Joseph Mackert!" I had rarely heard my mother yell the way she did that day. "You get down off that horse this instant!"

Then she calmed down enough to realize that screaming at me might startle me into falling. With all the reserve she could muster, Mom congratulated me on the new trick and asked me to have a seat on the horse for a moment. As soon as I was safely seated, she instructed me that while the stunt was a good show of horsemanship, it was also far too dangerous and I was forbidden to attempt it again. Of course, to a young boy, that simply meant I had given my mother the scare of her life and the whole thing was well executed. If the opportunity presented itself, I knew I would do it again. And imagine what my brothers would think!

Butch became a great playmate for Mark and me. When we had to irrigate the pastures, we would ride him at full gallop through the ditches with water splashing all over the place. We dropped out of trees onto Butch's back, jumped off the haystack onto his back, leapfrogged over Butch's hindquarters onto his back, practiced falling from his back at full gallop—we did it all. Butch was our faithful steed no matter where our imaginations took us. He was our proof that we were growing into men. He was the evidence that we could do something that would impress our older brothers. His own mother didn't want him, and his human owner had accepted that he would not survive. But he had survived, and I admired him for that. I had envied our old cow Brown Sugar for her ability to receive the affection she wanted, and I admired Butch's will to survive when the people who should have cared most about him didn't.

I loved that horse! At night when we milked the cows and fed Butch, I would stand at the feeding trough and comb the manure out of his coat. To this day I can't help thinking about Butch whenever I catch the scent of horse dander.

BANDIT WAS another of God's creatures that entered my life at a point when I needed some devoted affection. One year when I was about nine, a stray female dog, some kind of Labrador mix, was hanging around our property looking for food. She seemed to make her home in the neighbor's junkyard behind our house and sometimes rooted through our trash. As spring rolled around, we realized she was pregnant and later, when I noticed her belly had shrunk, I knew the pups had to be nearby. I kept an eye on that dog for a few days, and eventually I saw the hole in the boards where she was coming and going from the junkyard.

I grabbed Mark, and lickety-split, we were through that hole in the fence and into the junkyard on a mission. A few minutes later we were inside an old shed, and there were the puppies. With awe and wonder, we watched them sleep, their little chests rising and falling in rapid rhythm. We knew they were too little to play with, but at least now we knew where they were. The dog seemed to accept our presence as we visited frequently, and we reveled in watching the pups clamber to nurse and snuggle against her belly.

After awhile we noticed one little guy in particular. His size left him disadvantaged when it came to fighting to nurse. I once reached in and removed one of the largest pups and set the runt at a nipple. All the puppies had brown eyes except the runt. His were blue, and Mark and I couldn't help but fall in love with those beautiful blue puppy dog eyes. We began plotting how we might be able to acquire a couple of these puppies for ourselves. The runt was our favorite, and since we couldn't agree whom he should belong to, we decided that if we could get permission to have two dogs, we would just choose the two we liked best and raise them together.

We knew we had to start with our mothers. They both told us it didn't make sense to ask for a dog if we didn't know if the owner of the junkyard would give us one. The dog wasn't his, but the litter was born on his property, so that gave him some rights, apparently. So, we talked to Mr. Hyde about the puppies in the shed, and he said we could have two puppies, but we had to wait until they were six weeks old. At that point our mothers caved—but we still had to convince Father that we deserved the dogs. We choked on the lumps in our throats. How in the world were we going to convince Father that we were worthy of dogs?

I knew how hard Father was to please. I remembered a time when I was six when I cleaned up my room all by myself. This was a pretty serious spring-cleaning effort by a little boy. Nothing in my room was out of place. Mom was proud of the job I had done, so she went and got Father and asked him to inspect my room. Father came in, looked around, and agreed it was a thorough job of cleaning. Then he pointed to the bed and said that I could have made the bed tighter, and that when he was in the army his drill instructor would command them to remake the bed over and over again until it was so tight the drill instructor could bounce a quarter off it. Father also looked under my bed and said, "Ah, a ghost turd." I asked what that was, and he showed me the ball of dust that had formed under the bed.

I was stung that after all my hard work Father couldn't just say I had done a good job. Instead, he had to find something wrong. So I stripped my bed, cleaned the "ghost turds" out from under the bed and changed the quilt to something less fluffy. I made my bed and climbed under it to pull on the ends of the sheets and quilt until they were as tight as I could possibly get them. I didn't have a quarter, so I went into the utility room and punched out the round disks from an unused wall outlet box. A disk weighed close enough to a quarter and was about the same size and shape. I ran to my room and flipped the disk into the air. It bounced about three inches up off the quilt.

Ecstatic, I ran upstairs and invited Mom to come to my room and see something. I showed Mom that my bed was tight enough to bounce a quarter-sized piece of metal off it and asked if she had a real quarter to see if it would work. She said, "I think your father might have one." I grinned from ear to ear. She went upstairs with me scrambling right behind her and asked Father to come and take a look at my bed again. When he protested, she said, "You really need to see this, Clyde."

Father came down into my room and I said, "Father, get a quarter and see if it will bounce off the bed." Father smiled and pulled a quarter out of his pocket and placed it on his thumb, ready to flip it onto the bed. I held my breath as it sailed through the air. It hit the bed and popped up into the air about five inches off the bed. Father was impressed. "Well, son, that's as good as any bed I ever made when I was in the army," he said as he messed up my hair. "You've done a good job. The next question is, can you make your bed that well every morning?"

I assured him that I could, and my face beamed as he left my room. I continued to make my bed like that for about three months, every day hoping that this would be the day Father would come and see my accomplishment. He never did. Father wasn't paying attention. He was never going to look at my bed again; he didn't care how hard I was working to please him. I gave up making my bed.

Knowing from the past how difficult it was to please Father, how was I going to impress him enough this time that he would let me have a puppy?

When Father came home that night, Mark and I made sure we had his slippers in hand, waiting for him to sit down in his favorite chair to watch TV. Our hearts pounded as I unzipped Father's boots to remove them and Mark handed him the remote control. Once Father was comfortable with the slippers on, we asked if we could get him something to drink.

"Some ice water would be nice," he said.

Both of us shot off to the kitchen to fetch the water. Then we got out Father's shoeshine box, sat on the floor beside his chair on newspaper to protect the carpet, and went to work on his boots. We finished one pair, and I went to the closet for another. While we buffed, Mark and I laughed when Father laughed, expressed disgust when he was disgusted, and complained when he complained. After an hour of this, I nudged Mark and he nudged me back. We argued with our eyes about who should broach the subject with Father. Finally I mustered my courage—at the next commercial break. Talking during a TV show was a sure way to get a fast no. Father would disappear into the living room to watch TV as soon as he came home from work. He wouldn't even leave long enough to come and eat dinner with the rest of us. He claimed that he gave up eating with us because we were such disgusting pigs that it made him sick to sit at the table with us. I only remember two occasions in my childhood when Father ate at the dinner table with the family when it wasn't Thanksgiving or some other holiday. I hoped a commercial would come before I lost my nerve.

Finally the commercials came. With fire in my gut, I managed to say, "Father, when you have a minute, Mark and I would like to talk to you about something."

"Did you do something wrong?" That was the first thought that sprang to his mind.

"No!" I exclaimed. "We just need to ask you something."

"Okay," he said. "When Mother Donna calls you for dinner, run in there and get me my tray. We'll talk after dinner."

So far so good. Mark and I held up crossed fingers. We delivered Father's tray and rushed through our own food and headed back to the living room. It wasn't long before his program came to an end; this was our chance.

"Come into the study," he said. We followed close behind, our stomachs in our throats.

I took a deep breath and plunged in. "Mr. Hyde has a dog that has a litter of new puppies and he said we could have two if we want them and if you let us have them we can train them to help on the farm and they can protect the house and the family from burglars and they will keep weasels out of the chicken coops and keep them safe and it would be really neat to have a dog, don't you think?" I ran out of breath and had to stop.

"How old are these puppies?" Father asked. "And are they old enough to be taken from their mother?"

"They will be in two more weeks," Mark answered.

"What do your mothers think?"

We'd done our homework on that front. "They both said it was up to you, Father." We held our breath.

"Well, if you want a dog, you have to earn it. You have to prove you're responsible."

Our hearts leaped out of our chests; there was hope!

"For the next two weeks, you have to be on your best behavior. I want all your chores done on time and without complaint. You also have to do extra chores, and I want a freshly shined pair of boots ready for me every morning. Your mothers will give you the rest of the chores. If I get one bad report, that's it, no dog. Do you understand?"

Father could have told us to fly to the moon and back, and we would have found a way.

For the next two weeks we were on our extra best behavior. We were kind to our siblings, did our chores on time, asked for extra chores, and made sure every pair of Father's boots was shined so that it didn't matter what he decided to wear. After two weeks we reminded Father that we'd done everything he asked of us. Our mothers gave a good report. The end result was that Father said we could get one dog to share.

We had focused so much on the possibility that he might say no that it hadn't occurred to us that Father would cut our request in half. It was better than no puppy, so we heartily agreed, thanking him repeatedly as we walked backward and bowed as we left. We shot off on a dead run to let Mr. Hyde know Father had given his permission. At the shed we found some of the puppies were already gone, and our hearts nearly stopped. But there he was; there was no question which puppy we wanted. We picked up the runt and carried him home.

We named him Bandit and immediately implemented a training program. We taught him the usual obedience behaviors, such as "sit," "stay," "lie," "come," "beg," and "shake hands," but we also taught him games that entertained us. We'd sneak him into the boys' end of the house through the basement windows and sit in the hall facing each other, tossing a tennis ball back and forth and watching him go nuts trying to capture the ball.

Life was heaven with Bandit around. My brother Paul was in the middle of a rebellious stage by then, at age sixteen. He defied many of Father's rules and pretty much did whatever he wanted, and that included getting a puppy for himself. So we ended up with two after all. Bandit and Herk jumped across the irrigation ditches to stay with us, they conspired with us against our sisters' cats, and they played every game we teased them with.

The Fourth of July was coming up, and the family was planning a day at the baseball field with a picnic. We always enjoyed playing softball together; anything that involved sports was another opportunity to shine and be noticed by Father. The night before, we took Bandit out to the dog run and settled him in for the night before turning in ourselves.

Mark and I woke in the morning to the sound of puppy paws clawing at the bedroom window. Bandit and Herk had found a way out of the dog run; they knew our window well because we'd snuck them in that way many times. We played with them for a moment, and then set them outside while we ran upstairs to gather what we needed to milk the cows. Heading out the back door, we looked both ways to check for cars—and that's when we saw the black lump lying at the side of the road. It could only be one of the dogs; I prayed it wasn't Bandit.

It was.

It wasn't all right to cry, so I held it all in as Mark and I picked up our puppy's body and carried it into the barn with us. I buried my head in the cow's flank just like always, but this time I let my tears slide into the milk bucket. It was the only place I could cry and no one would see. When we were finished milking, we dug our dog's grave.

Ken came out to the graveside to see us. "Father wants to know if you guys are coming with us."

It had never occurred to us we might be allowed to stay home alone while the family went to the Fourth of July festivities.

"Father said to tell you that if you want to stay here today, you can. But it's one or the other. You either come now or stay home all day and miss everything."

I looked at Mark, and he looked at me. We stayed home that day. We laid on our bellies under the shade of the tree next to Bandit's open grave with one hand stroking his fur. We told stories about all the fun we had and his courageous battles with the cat. When we ran out of stories, we cried. We just laid there in the shade of the tree and cried. Everything bottled up inside us by the house rules and regulations came flooding out.

Bandit was our dog, something of our own. We didn't share him with anybody. He wasn't handed down from anybody. We'd trained him ourselves. We didn't have to do anything to earn his affection. We just loved him, and he loved us. When we lost Bandit, we lost an experience of unconditional love we had never known before.

MARK AND I loved to sleep outside in the summer and used any excuse we could to drag a mattress outside and spend the night under the stars. Our best hope for receiving the answer we wanted was on nights when we had to get the irrigation water in the middle of the night. We justified this to Mother Donna by explaining that if we slept outside, we wouldn't wake anyone in the house with our alarm clock or as we left the house and came back later. We had to ask permission each time; just because she let us do it once didn't mean she would let us do it

again. Of course, if she said we couldn't sleep outside, we made sure
that the back door slammed pretty good on our way out and again on
our way back in. If we did this, generally she was more inclined to say
yes the next time. We went around this loop a number of times in the
summer—asking permission, being denied, proving our point, getting
permission the next time, then once again being denied.

Because we lived far from the lights of Salt Lake City in an area of
Sandy that hadn't been developed yet, the stars were brilliantly visible at
night. Sleeping out under the stars became a spooky event when the older
kids started telling stories about UFOs. Every night during the summer
we'd stare up at the sky for hours, hoping to get a glimpse of UFOs.
The older siblings assured Mark and me they were shaped like birds and
glowed with a bluish white light. They also moved swiftly across the sky
without a sound from engines manufactured in another world.

One night when Mark and I were outside, the sun had just set
and the stars were out. The dim lights of Sandy fought feebly against
the darkening sky glimmering at us with a starry sense of the vast
unknown. We laid out the mattresses and went inside to get blankets
and pillows. As we came back outside, I noticed a bluish white light in
the shape of a bird moving silently across the sky. Chills shot down my
spine. I couldn't believe it; I had spotted the UFOs! They had revealed
themselves to me! I ran back inside yelling, "The UFOs are back!"
The older kids came pouring out of the house and saw the lights too.
We all stood there in amazement; this was a historic moment in our
family.

"Wait a minute!" I exclaimed. In a flash, I saw the truth. "Those
aren't UFOs. Those are ducks flying north, and the lights from the city
are shining off of the oil on their feathers!"

Mark mumbled, "Well, they were UFOs until you identified them."

Lying in the backyard, I would look up at the stars and contemplate the expanse of the universe and consider the God who created it. I thought of all the other gods out there who had progressed to godhood and created their own worlds. Would I be able to join them one day and create my own world to rule over? I pondered the things my parents taught me about God and wondered if he really existed. I wanted to believe everything my parents taught me. I wanted to believe the teachings of the FLDS Church. I wanted to be sure I was on the path to godhood and that someday I would grow up to be a god who ruled his own kingdom. I knew I didn't want to face damnation, so the only option was to stay on the straight and narrow path the FLDS Church laid out in front of me.

However, periodically I was seized with doubt. Seeing all the stars and imagining faraway worlds where UFOs might come from, I wondered if we were really alone in the universe. It was no conundrum to believe there was a God who created all of this; that was no puzzle for me. God creating the world made perfect sense. But if he created us, then why couldn't he create other races on other worlds as well? If he was really God, couldn't he do that? At the root of my ponderings was whether or not God was the God that was explained to me as a child. Were we right in the FLDS Church? Of all the people in the world, were we really the only ones who had the truth? If the truth of plural marriage was so great, and if it was the only way to a celestial kingdom, then why didn't others know the truth? Why were we the outcasts who had to live secretly?

Lying out there surveying the stars, I felt small and insignificant. I was one of thirty-one children who would populate my father's celestial kingdom; my significance derived from what my existence meant for my father. The mothers, whose salvation depended on my father's godhood, exhausted themselves just keeping us fed and clothed and not killing each other. My father was distant and didn't involve himself in our daily doings unless he was inclined to exercise control in some way.

So I wondered, *If I didn't matter to anyone else, did I really matter to God?*

7

Hormones and Heaven

*The only men who become Gods, even the Sons
of God, are those who enter into polygamy.*

—Brigham Young, Journal of Discourses,
August 19, 1866, vol. 11, p. 269

From the time I was small, I knew that someday I was to be a god. This was at the heart of the priesthood hierarchy that began in the family and progressed through the FLDS Church. This was motivation for righteous living. Life for a man was about being worthy to progress toward being a god, and I had been privileged to be born into the faithful who could hold the priesthood.

I learned very early that before the world began, God—who had once been a man—lived in heaven with his many goddess wives. Through them he had many spirit-children who didn't yet have bodies. In order to progress to godhood, God's children had to receive physical bodies like the one God has. So God planned to send them down to the earth he was going to create. They would receive their physical bodies and go through the tests and trials of the flesh. Only when they had learned to subdue the flesh would they be able to progress to godhood and become like God their Father.

But God needed a plan for man's salvation, because in physical form his children would fall into a sinful state. God called together a council of gods and asked his two oldest children, Jesus and Lucifer, for suggestions. Lucifer jumped in with a plan to force man to obey God's laws and bring back all of God's children. He wanted the glory for himself for accomplishing such a feat. Jesus, the firstborn, suggested God give humans freedom to choose whether or not to obey, and that he would go down and die for their sins. Those who believed would obey God because they loved him. God would only get back those who were worthy to progress to godhood. Jesus wanted all the glory to go to God. The council voted and accepted Jesus' plan.

Lucifer was furious! He began to sow discord among God's spirit-children until he had convinced a third of them to revolt against God. War broke out in heaven, and Lucifer was defeated and cast down with his hordes to earth without physical bodies. On earth, they would continue to try and tempt the souls of men to revolt against God.

Another third of the hosts of heaven had not been able to make up their minds which side to fight on, or had been cowards and not fought valiantly. These spirits were allowed to receive a physical body through which they could progress to godhood in the next life. However, they were not allowed to hold the authority of God's priesthood—the power and authority to act on God's behalf on earth. They were cursed with a dark skin as a reminder concerning the holding of the priesthood. This is why, historically, black males were not allowed to hold the priesthood in the Mormon faith. The FLDS Church considers the 1978 decision of the LDS Church revoking the curse a compromise of the truth.

The last third of the hosts of heaven sided with Jesus and God the Father and fought valiantly. They were granted the right to come to earth and receive a physical body through which they, too, could progress to godhood. Because they acted with honor on God's behalf in heaven, they also were allowed to hold the priesthood to act on God's behalf on earth. They would be born into the physical realm with bodies that were white and delightsome.

According to the laws and ordinances of Mormonism, only through righteous living can a man eventually progress to godhood, where he will become a god in his own right. As gods, men will parent their own spirit-children and create and rule over their own planets, just as God created earth and rules over it. "As man is, God once was; as God is, man may become" was the teaching pressed into me at every opportunity.

Added to this was Joseph Smith's teaching that only men with three wives could become gods. Joseph Smith used this doctrine to convince women they were supposed to be his spiritual wives despite already being married to living husbands. This was the very heart of why the fundamentalist polygamists had rejected the mainline LDS effort to eschew polygamy. Without plural marriage, there could be no godhood. So even as children, we began to think about marriage.

About the time that my oldest sisters, Connie and Carole, were of marriageable age, Uncle Roy received a revelation from God about a new law called the Law of Placing. Uncle Roy simply expanded on the teaching of Joseph Smith. In order to ensure that the right couples were married to each other here on earth, the Priesthood Council—specifically Uncle Roy—would match each couple through the same kind of revelation from God that Joseph Smith claimed to have received. The girls knew they would be given to a man whom the Priesthood Council chose. Things were a little iffier for boys. Obviously, plural marriage does not require as many males as females, so the older we boys got, the more we realized we had to prove ourselves worthy of being given our wives.

Dating in the FLDS was prohibited. After all, there was no need to get to know the person you married before the ceremony; the Apostles had received a divine revelation that you should marry this person, or you wouldn't be at the wedding in the first place. Your job was to be worthy of the wives you would be given, not to worry about finding them or falling in love.

But even polyg kids have hormones. The Law of Placing didn't keep teenagers from feeling attractions and wondering about love.

BOYS WERE not allowed to talk to girls on the phone. To elude this rule, boys enlisted sisters as liaisons. A sister would call the girl a boy had his eye on. Girls calling girls would not raise suspicions on the other end of the phone. However, once the adored girl was on the phone, the besotted boy would grab the phone from the sister and strike up a conversation. It might not last long, but it was sheer joy at the time. Another strategy was to befriend a girl's brother and enlist his help. If the girl happened to go to our school, things were much easier because not every moment of the school day was strictly guarded. Mother Donna just didn't have that many eyes!

Whatever the strategy, boys managed to send messages to girls that they would be at certain places at certain times of the night, and both boys and girls would sneak away for stolen dates.

My brothers Steve and Ken had crushes on Wendy and Naomi Millsap, so whenever the occasion came up to run an errand (whether real or manufactured), they would drive by the Millsap house. Many times they would drive by just to see if they could catch a glimpse of one of these fair maidens. For some strange reason, I grew up thinking that every destination involved driving past Brother Millsap's house! Steve did end up marrying Naomi Millsap; apparently he proved himself worthy of her in the end. Stan's attentions shifted to Valerie Jeffs, the daughter of Apostle Rulon Jeffs and sister of Warren Jeffs. Stan and Valerie arranged many late-night rendezvous, desperately hoping but never being sure if ultimately they would be chosen for each other. In the end they were allowed to marry.

A girl's greatest fear was to marry out of obligation to enter into the principle of plural marriage without hope of love. Of course, the principle trumped any other factors at play, because, without plural marriage, the only destiny was damnation. Girls knew they had to be married; they could not achieve salvation on their own. But deep down, they wanted to be wooed. Girls had three chances to marry someone they loved.

The first hope was to be the first wife, the first woman the husband loved, his first sexual encounter. Even when the husband took another wife—as demanded by FLDS doctrine to avoid eternal damnation—no one could usurp the status of a first wife. The first sexual relationship could only happen once. And there was always the possibility that a bride would grow to love her husband, even if she didn't when they married. That was risky; there were no guarantees, but if you were the first wife, the odds were better of forming a love attachment than if you were a later wife.

The second hope for love was to be the favorite wife. Girls liked to believe that it was possible to become the favorite wife even if the husband already had several others. Most young women ended up married to someone they didn't love and barely knew because of the obligation to plural marriage. A second or third wife would try that much harder to please her husband, hoping against hope that he would come to see her with greater favor than the others, especially the first wife. A second or third—or fourth or fifth or sixth or seventh—wife might use her youthful assets in the bed-room or excel at managing tasks around the household or strive to have the most appealing personality of the wives.

For the most part, the future of these girls was grim; they knew they were likely to marry without love and out of obligation to the principle and quite possibly to an older man. The truth was, a stolen teenage romance might be their only hope to taste love for themselves. A woman would always have the memory of the boy who chased her when they were teens. None of my full-blooded sisters married their sweethearts. My sisters Rena and Kathy were married against their will to my stepbrothers, Mother Maurine's sons John and Daniel. Mary was married off to an older man who was a complete stranger. Laura did not marry a man she loved, but she at least married a man she chose for herself whom she felt she might grow to love.

Some girls held out for the only other option: Find a boy, fall in love, and run away with him. This was risky because the FLDS didn't like letting girls leave. Boys were more dispensable, but the community needed the girls to be plural wives so the men could earn their godhood and populate their kingdoms. Many girls who tried to run away—with or without a boy—were brought back under the authority of the law as a runaway without much investigation by outside law enforcement into why the girl fled in the first place. This was especially true of girls run-ning from the Short Creek community that straddled Hildale, Utah, and Colorado City, Arizona. The police there were all polygamists, and they promptly returned the girls they caught, as well as cooperating with other communities from which girls had fled. In the area around Salt Lake City, however, the rate at which girls were returned was far lower since the polygamists did not dominate local government. Nevertheless, some girls were caught and returned by other means.

These runaways didn't have a prayer once they were returned. They would be married off promptly to keep them from running again. Once married, they were likely to be pregnant before long, and that would make contemplating flight far more complex. Where would they go? How would they earn a living in the outside world with only a sixth- or eighth-grade education and no employable job skills? How would they provide for children on their own? To survive, they'd have to leave their children behind, and it was rare for a woman to be willing to do that.

If a girl made it to the age of eighteen without being married and chose to run, she couldn't legally be brought back against her will. So the Apostles employed threat and intimidation, dangling their eternal salvation in front of them. If a girl didn't return, she would face damnation. Without becoming a plural wife, she could not be saved and live in the celestial kingdom. If that wasn't enough to convince her to return, she was reminded of Brigham Young's doctrine of "blood atonement." Some sins were beyond the redemptive power of the blood of Christ. The individual had to shed his or her own blood in order to atone. This atonement could be either voluntary or involuntary—it didn't really matter. So, out of fear for their daughter's eternal damnation, it was better for the family to "blood atone" her than to let her suffer in hell for eternity. Girls who left the community risked the threat of involuntary blood atonement—throats slit from ear to ear, or bellies ripped open. Faced with this, many runaways returned. Rumors circulated steadily of deaths that happened by blood atonement but were covered up by an accident of some kind. We had no way to know if these accounts were true; quite possibly they were manufactured to frighten other young women. What may simply have been a successful getaway was reported as blood atonement and turned into propaganda to control and frighten others.

But we could never be sure. What if it were true?

A BOY could possibly marry the girl he loved as his first wife. In our family, three of my brothers married their sweethearts—Phillip, Stan, and Steve. If that didn't happen, the backup plan wasn't as bleak for boys as it was for girls. A man had the opportunity to marry more than one woman—at least three was the goal. It was possible that one of his wives might help him forget the girl who caught his eye as a young man. Or the woman he had his eye on might become a second or third wife. For many men, though, the women simply became tools for building the kingdom on earth. After all, collecting multiple wives was all about establishing your own kingdom for the next life.

However, in general, the path to marriage was much harder for boys than for girls. In order to have enough women to go around, the system had to eliminate the competition among the men. So the FLDS leadership made it an intricate process for young men to progress to the point where they were considered worthy of receiving one of the daughters of the congregation. In reality, it wasn't merely a matter of being a good man, of knowing the rules and playing fair. It was political, it was religious subjugation, and often it was unseen forces operating against you. The goal was to make it so hard for the less-desirable young men to be worthy that they would despair and leave on their own. If they weren't smart enough to figure that out, they were escorted out by one means or another, becoming one of the "lost boys" of the FLDS. So if you had any hope of marrying someone you loved, first you had to make it through the attempts to weed you out, and then you had to be lucky enough that the girl you loved was not already married off to someone else before you were worthy. Being young and single didn't mean you had priority over older men who had several wives already. In fact, it was quite the opposite; these older men had already proven themselves worthy to receive multiple wives, and they were older and further along in their journey toward godhood. The competition, though unspoken, was pervasive and fierce. It was enough to make anyone give up hope. Faced with the prospect of never being deemed worthy, many boys apostatized—left the FLDS knowing they were walking away from eternal salvation.

As boys approached puberty, they began to realize that the road to salvation was much wider for women than for men. True, women needed the men to be saved. But several women could participate in salvation by being married to one man. Mathematically it was impossible for there to be enough women within the community for all the men to have plural wives. So the young men who realized they were never going to be worthy didn't have much to lose when they left the FLDS. If they were excluded from salvation and faced damnation anyway, they might as well enjoy all the forbidden activities—drinking, drugs, sex, and so on. In utter hopelessness, many lives spun into disaster. Boys and young men ended up on the streets of a city outside the community—homeless, broke, addicted to drugs and alcohol. They had only a sixth- or eighth-grade education and no particular skills. Some learned farming or construction, but generally they ended up in dead-end, low-paying jobs.

The motivation that brought boys and girls out to meet each other at night isn't hard to understand. The only hope for both eternal salvation and happiness was to be married to someone you loved. Both the future life and the present life were at stake. So the girls would sneak out at night to meet a potential love whom they dreamed of marrying one day, hoping that when the time came, Uncle Roy would receive the revelation that they should be together.

Now, if a woman went to the Priesthood Council and said she felt she was supposed to marry a certain man, they often gave her to that man— unless she was desired by another man who held higher social or political standing in the FLDS. A man could likewise go and ask for a specific girl and tell the council he felt she was right for him. The Priesthood Council might or might not agree to a union a young man requested. The simple fact is there weren't enough women to go around, so they had to exclude some of the boys to be able to marry girls off to men who had already proven themselves. That meant saying no most of the time.

Position in the community trumped everything. If Uncle Roy's favorite son fancied a girl, he was going to get that girl. Everyone else would conveniently be considered unworthy of her, no matter what. The politics were complex at times, with competition for standing and recognition among the men, but the long and the short of it was that women were bartered with. The more daughters you had to offer to the system, the better your chances of advancing your position. The standing of the men is what mattered; how the girls felt was trivial. As horrifying as it sounded, many girls were given in marriage to men who were the same age or older than their own fathers—and many of the fathers were older than the typical father in American society in the first place because the girls might be the youngest children of younger wives.

As a young girl, my sister Mary was in love with John Swaney, our stepbrother (Mother Maurine's son). She wanted to marry him, but Father considered him unworthy of the match and a flight risk. The last thing you wanted to do was marry off your daughter to a man who was likely to apostatize and take her with him. As much as she cared for John, Mary was pressed into agreeing that John might want to leave the community; she couldn't risk her eternal salvation by marrying him. Mary's heart had been broken by the disqualifying of her first love, and quite soon she was married off to Bill Draper, a much older man who already had five wives and would take a seventh after Mary. She resigned herself to the life chosen for her by religious leaders and parents.

Mary later described her wedding day as the saddest say of her life. She left everything she loved to go away with a strange man thirty-three years older than she was. There was a thunderstorm that day, and she sat in the car with our parents, praying for a tree to fall on her so she could die. She begged God to take her away. But by the end of the day she was married and gone from us. When she married Draper, Mary became a "poofer," a girl who disappeared without a trace.

Mary's marriage to Draper was a secret within the community and even within her own family. We were not allowed to know where she was or even, at the time, to whom she was married. All that Mom would tell us was that Mary had been married to a prominent man. Mary wasn't allowed to go to the church services or be seen in public where anyone in the group might be able to associate her with our family or with being Draper's sixth wife. Several years passed before the rest of the family had any idea where she was.

I was only a year and a half old when Mary left; Mary was seventeen. She had practically raised me in my infancy, taking care of me while Mom worked long hours. Though I wasn't allowed to see Mary after her marriage, as I grew up, Mom told me stories about Mary and how much she loved me and mothered me. Mom would show me pictures of Mary, and I would stare at them for hours, trying to remember the sister I never really knew, the one who mothered me and loved me in a way the rest of the family seemed incapable of. Even though I didn't remember Mary, because of my mother's stories I resented that she had been taken from me and longed for the day I would be able to see her again. That day didn't come for ten years.

Interestingly enough, while my stepbrother John was disqualified from marrying Mary, he was approved as a husband for my sister Rena. It made no sense. Why would he be less of a flight risk married to Rena instead of Mary, whom he loved? It was just another control game. Mary loved John; Rena detested him. There wasn't another soul on the face of the earth she loathed more. So, naturally, John was selected as the one Rena should spend eternity with. She didn't have a choice. Mary was sent away brokenhearted, and Rena was forced to submit to a man she hated. Whatever you wanted was the one thing that would be withheld from you—lest you begin to think you had the least bit of control over your own life.

In some situations, teenagers became too intimately involved with each other—or at least it had been rumored that they had. But even being sexually involved wasn't a guarantee that you would be allowed to marry the person you chose. Many girls swore they would only marry their sweethearts, but even if they had been sexually involved, when the Priesthood Council applied pressure, the girls didn't have the intestinal fortitude to suggest that the council, or even their parents, had received an erroneous revelation. The issue at stake was eternal salvation, not just for the girls, but for their whole families. This was another technique modeled by Joseph Smith, who linked entering plural marriage to assuring salvation not just for the women but for her whole family as well. If a girl in our community tried to defy the Priesthood Council, her whole family's salvation was endangered. That was a tremendous weight to put on a young girl who only wanted to be happy.

My brother Paul tried romancing a girl with the hope she would marry him rather than the man the Priesthood Council had chosen for her. Her name was Joyce. She promised she would never marry anyone else, but she ended up breaking Paul's heart.

Before getting involved with Joyce, Paul had a relationship with another polyg girl. They went as far as heavy kissing and petting; she was a virgin and didn't want to go further. They separated for the time being, but several years later Paul ran into her and she was all over him, and the two of them did have a sexual relationship. In the years in between, the young woman had become sexually active and at one point had sex with a black man—a Negro from the cursed race of Cain. Some have argued that the sexual encounter with the black man was consensual, while others argued she was raped. Ferreting out the truth didn't matter to Uncle Roy. Paul had had sex with a woman who willingly or unwillingly had sex with the seed of Cain, and therefore, both she and Paul were now cursed. Fundamentalists believe the teachings of the early Mormon leaders who espoused that marrying into or having a sexual relationship with someone who is of the cursed seed of Cain brought with it spiritual death and the inability to ever hold the priesthood in this life. The curse was passed from one generation to the next and through sexual relations.

Paul would never hold the priesthood in this life. He was not eligible to receive any daughters from within the group as a wife. This all came to light when Paul wanted to marry Joyce.

The Priesthood Council presented Joyce to another man they wanted her to marry. She was forced to face her prejudices against the black race, which now included Paul. Despite her promises to Paul, she couldn't risk her salvation or the salvation of her family, and she accepted the choice the council made for her. The wedding was arranged quickly, and Joyce was married before Paul could plead his case. Uncle Roy purposely would not give Paul an audience until after Joyce was married, so all Paul could do was register his complaint.

Logic had no part in any of this.

When Paul learned the reason he had been disqualified—being cursed with Negro blood—he had the gall to point out to Uncle Roy that our Father had slept with a Puerto Rican woman while he was in the army and stationed in her country. This would have contaminated Father and all his children. The lack of logic came into play because Uncle Roy was married to my sister Carole. He was seventy-two and she was seventeen when they married. By his own logic, Carole was contaminated because of Father's relationship with the woman in Puerto Rico, and if Uncle Roy was her husband, then he was cursed as well. So how was he any different than Paul?

Uncle Roy, being fully confident in his position as Prophet, simply dismissed this line of reasoning and claimed, "It didn't work that way." Somehow he and Carole were immune to the curse, but Paul had not been lucky enough to elude it.

Paul eventually was driven from the community with a broken heart. There was no one to stand up for him, least of all Father. Our father had his own standing to worry about; he couldn't challenge the authorities, even if he'd wanted to, without risk that he would be declared unworthy and his own wives would be stripped away from him. But even apart from these risks to himself, Father didn't show interest in resolving Paul's dilemma. Marrying off the girl a young man loved produced such resentment toward the leadership that the young man couldn't possibly stay in the community. Despite the machinations of leadership, technically Paul's departure was voluntary; he was one less buck to compete against the herd for the does, leaving more women available for the worthy men.

Both Phillip and Stan, sons of Mother Midge, married their sweethearts, who were both daughters of the Apostle and Priesthood Council member Rulon Jeffs—despite our father's escapades in Puerto Rico. Paul was not worthy of the girl he loved, but Phillip and Stan, sons of a man who had committed the same sin, were worthy of the daughters of an Apostle. The contradictions were glaring, but consistency wasn't the issue. Power was. Control was. Rank was. Phil and Stan were sons of a first wife, and their wives were daughters of an Apostle. Paul was the son of a third wife. He was nothing. He was expendable, even to his own father.

One of the other ways of driving a young man away was to tell him to marry a woman no one wanted. One sure way to test the resolve or loyalties of a young man was to match him with a girl who revolted him. If a man had the courage to refuse a daughter of the community who was offered to him, it meant going to the back of the line. He would have to wait until all the other men were matched or disqualified before being considered again. There was always the risk that this move would bring such scrutiny of the man that he would end forfeiting his chance of any future match. The alternative was to marry an unappealing woman with the hope that he would do better the next time around.

This happened to my brother Howard, who was ordered to marry a woman who was not at all desirable to him. Out of obligation to the principle, he married her, knowing that he would have to wait even longer to ever have another opportunity to marry. If he refused, the Priesthood Council might well never consider him a worthy candidate for one of the daughters of the community. Howard and David were married at the same time but couldn't have been further apart in their reactions. David was a giddy newlywed, but Howard looked like a man who had eaten his last meal and faced nothing but death. In the meantime, he could hope that he would somehow learn to love this woman, that God would somehow make her beautiful in his eyes. In the end, though, Howard couldn't bring himself to consummate the union. After less than four months of marriage, he sent her back to her family and apostatized from the faith. He knew he'd used up his last chance to be considered worthy. We all mourned the loss of Howard to the fold and feared for his mortal soul.

IN MANY cases, if a young man's family wasn't prominent enough, if he was considered a flight risk, or if he was disqualified for any reason, the standard response was to tell him that there weren't enough women to go around. If he wanted a wife, he would have to go out into the world and convert someone to the principle of plural marriage. In this modern day, that would be like finding the thinnest of needles in the biggest of haystacks. Any young woman who would agree to such an arrangement had to have serious emotional issues. Theoretically it would be easier to convert someone from the mainstream LDS by convincing her that the Manifesto that distanced the Mormons from polygamy in 1890 had just been a ruse to acquire statehood for Utah and was not spiritually binding. Even in the LDS world, though, we were like lepers. They didn't associate with us any more than mainstream U.S. culture did. Mormons wished we weren't around to remind them of the polygamist roots of their faith. It would have been much easier to convince a polyg girl to run away than convert an LDS girl to our leper colony.

So boys continued to sneak out to meet girls at night, all of them knowing that their chances of marrying for love were slim, but dreaming the dreams of youth that perhaps they would be the exception to the rule.

8

Burning in the Bosom

Little children are whole, for they are not capable of
committing sin ... Behold I say unto you that this
thing shall ye teach—repentance and baptism unto
those who are accountable and capable of committing
sin; yea, teach parents that they must repent and
be baptized, and humble themselves as their little
children, and they shall all be saved with their little
children. And their little children need no repentance,
neither baptism ... But little children are alive in
Christ, even from the foundation of the world.

—Book of Mormon, Moroni 8:8–12

I watched as Camille entered the baptismal waters with Father. After
safely positioning her so she would not strike her head on the edge of
the pool, he raised his massive right hand above his head.

"I baptize you in the name of the Father and the Son and the Holy
Ghost," Father proclaimed.

The next moment he laid Camille down into the water. I was there to observe Camille's baptism because I was the next in line to turn eight years old. Before long I would be expected to enter the water with Father to partake in this rite of passage, and Mark would be there to observe my baptism.

Later, both Mom and Father had a long talk with me about baptism. It was the next logical step in progressing to adulthood—and godhood—and I was painfully aware this step was crucial to my eternal salvation. My parents emphasized I should not enter into it lightly. I was coming up on the age when I would be held accountable for my sins. They assured me that so far in my life I was innocent before God. When I turned eight, I would enter into the age of accountability and God would judge me for my sins. After I was eight, my only hope for the remission of my sins was baptism by someone in authority.

In order to be baptized, I had to accept that the Mormon Church was God's one true church. We were taught that the mainstream LDS Church was originally God's one true church, but that it was out of order and in a state of apostasy. One day God would send a man prophesied as the "One Mighty and Strong" who would set the LDS Church in order before Christ's second coming. When that happens, the fundamentalists and the mainstream Mormons would be united again in one church and one brotherhood of believers. Being baptized would mean I believed all this. I also had to believe that the *Book of Mormon* was true, and that Joseph Smith was a true prophet of God. My parents told me I could know these things were true if I would earnestly pray, believing God would answer me. God would give me a "burning in the bosom" to confirm these truths. I had no reason to believe God would not give me this assurance. All of my older siblings had been through this already, and they all had received a testimony—a private revelation from the Holy Spirit through feelings and thoughts—that these things were true. Every one of them had been baptized. Why should it not happen to me as well?

About three months before my eighth birthday, with great anticipation I began to pray earnestly for the first time in my life. Until that time, prayer was something I did because I saw others doing it. I had never felt like my prayers ever went higher than the ceiling, but I reasoned that it was simply because I was an innocent child and therefore my prayers were just for practice. After all, what could an innocent child of God really need in conversing with the Almighty? Approaching baptism was a new and exciting time in my life. I was going to pray, and God was going to communicate to me his will and give me an unshakable testimony, a revelation, that would carry me through all the trials of life and bring me safely home again.

I read time and time again the story of Joseph Smith Jr. and how after reading from James 1:5 in the Bible, he believed God would give him wisdom. The *Book of Mormon* told how those who asked were promised they would receive a testimony of its truth. I began a heartfelt campaign to know for myself as my parents said I must. This was my moment of truth, and I embraced it with great excitement.

I prayed earnestly for God to give me a testimony. When I didn't immediately receive one, I went to my mother and asked her why I didn't have a burning in my bosom—a feeling of confirmation—yet. She explained that sometimes it takes a little while to get an answer to prayer; sometimes when we aren't sincere in our petitions before the Lord, he withholds the things we ask for until we pray truly believing he will answer. "God doesn't jump when we say jump," she explained. So I retired to the side of my bed to again petition God with all the earnestness of a seven-year-old for the truth to be revealed to me concerning Joseph Smith, the *Book of Mormon*, and the Mormon Church.

Nothing happened.

No lightning bolt, no opening skies, no burning in the bosom. Had I failed in being sincere when I prayed? Was there doubt in my heart hindering my petitions from being taken seriously by God? Was there sin in me preventing me from receiving a testimony—even though the *Book of Mormon* told me that I was yet without sin because I was still a child? Instead of assurance, anxiety mounted. I was eager to be done with this first obstacle in my spirituality. I wanted to join the ranks of those who had gone before me not just in my own immediate family but also for seven generations, all the way back to the days of Joseph Smith himself. Why wasn't I receiving a testimony?

Around this time I heard again the story of how God led the children of Israel out of the land of Egypt with his outstretched hand and how God hardened Pharaoh's heart. It seemed God had created Pharaoh for this purpose, and Pharaoh didn't have much choice in the matter. God hardened Pharaoh's heart to show Israel his mighty power. I began to wonder if God had predestined me as an agent of evil as well. No other explanation made sense.

I was running out of time! My siblings and parents were continually asking me, "Have you received an answer yet?" The sting of guilt slapped me every time someone asked. I had somehow fallen from God's good grace. How could God forsake me like this? How could I still be innocent before God, yet be abandoned in this silence? Eternity was closing in on me fast! I remembered all the teachings about those who are cast into outer darkness where there is wailing and gnashing of teeth, where the fire is never quenched and the worms don't die. This is the fate of those who reject the Mormon faith. With each passing day I felt the pressure increase to give Father an answer by my eighth birthday.

I knew one thing: I couldn't summon the courage to tell Father I hadn't received a testimony. I turned again to the only person I felt would help me without condemning me. I went to Mom and explained that I had tried, that I was sincere, that I prayed believing, but that I had not received my own testimony. I was in tears by the time I had blurted it all out. How I could bring myself to tell her I was sure I had been created as an agent of evil?

"What do you feel when you pray about these things?" Mom asked me.

I described the feelings I had, the churning of my stomach, the lump in my throat, the racing pulse—typical symptoms of anxiety.

Mom's eyes beamed and her face broke into a smile. "You've already received an answer, son," she announced. "You just didn't know how to describe it. That *is* the burning in the bosom, and Satan wants you to think it isn't real."

Apparently the puzzlement on my face had not escaped Mom's notice, because she nodded assurance that she was telling the truth. I couldn't break her heart and tell her I wasn't sure, while she stood there beaming with joy that now there was no obstacle to prevent her baby from entering the baptismal waters.

In that moment, a little boy decided to trust his mother's judgment on this matter; after all, she had experienced it before and knew what she was talking about. Rather than admit I was an agent of evil whom God was rejecting, that I was predestined for God's purpose to serve as a foe in his grand design, I opted for the more palatable answer my mother had provided me. But I sure didn't feel the relief I'd hoped for. Now I had another secret to carry.

"You need to go and tell Father you've received your answer and you want to be baptized," Mom said after a moment. "He will be very pleased to hear it from you."

Now the thought of going before Father and telling him I had received a testimony was a frightening prospect. Father was my priesthood head. God spoke directly to him and had charged him with my spiritual development and upbringing. Father was responsible before God to raise me in the "nurture and admonition of the Lord." Surely God would reveal to him that I wasn't certain, that I really didn't find out for myself, that I was racked with doubt. When Mom ushered me trembling before Father to announce that I had received my testimony, I was breathless with dread. I wanted to hide behind Mom and not have to face him. She ended up doing the talking—all the more reason to be certain Father would know I was a fraud.

"Is this true, son?" Father inquired.

I felt my throat swelling closed and couldn't push a sound through. I nodded my head to affirm the truth of my mother's explanation. The whole time I prayed that I wouldn't be discovered. A smile came across Father's face, and he placed his big hand on my shoulder.

"I'll take care of the arrangements," Father assured me. "I'm very proud of you."

I knew the touch of my father's disciplining hand; I was far less familiar with his touch of affection or approval. All my life I had wished for a father who noticed me. Now Father had touched me affectionately, and it was at my greatest moment of deceit so far. My baptism was enormously important to both of my parents. How could I ever speak the truth now?

With great relief, I left the room and finally had a sense of relative peace—after what I had just been through, anything outside the presence of my father could be considered peaceful. Surely Mom was right. Satan had tried to convince me that this wasn't a real testimony and that I was an agent of evil. Otherwise Father would have known the truth without my saying anything.

Father was true to his word and made all the arrangements. And as soon as I turned eight, Father baptized me in one of the most bizarre experiences of my life. In the locker room of a public hot-spring pool, I stood in shock as he began to strip off his clothes, not having a clue what to do myself. Modesty had always been paramount in our home. I wasn't sure if disrobing in front of Father was permitted or not. This was uncharted territory for me. By now Father was down to his briefs. I had never seen my father naked before and trembled at the thought that he would remove that last article of clothing.

Father looked over at me with an impatient glare. "What are you waiting for?" he snapped. "Get into your baptismal robe!"

Father and I entered the water together, and as we did, fear tightened its vice on me. When I came back up out of that water, I would be forever responsible and accountable to God for every sin I would ever commit from that moment on. I was wishing I had died in an accident before this moment arrived; it would have been much easier that way. I would have been blameless before God and would have gone straight into the kingdom to progress on to godhood without being subjected to temptations and sin. Perhaps Father would lose his grip on me and I would drown before he could regain it. But this wasn't my lucky day. Father invoked the names of the Mormon godhead and lowered me into the water. As I sputtered up again, I carried with me the terror of facing a world full of sin without the protection of youth to keep me innocent. For starters, was I now responsible for the lie I had told when I said I had received a testimony?

After my baptism came testimony Sunday. Being freshly dunked in the baptismal waters, I was expected to bear my testimony. This was the only course left for me; my only remaining hope was that my testimony was real but weak because it was a new one. Mother and Father both told me that the more I shared my testimony, the stronger it would become. I somehow made the connection with what they taught me about telling a lie—that if you tell it enough, eventually you will believe it yourself. From this moment on, I always had doubts about God and his existence as I wrestled with this internally, never daring to share my thoughts with anyone for fear of being found unworthy. So I bore my testimony, not because I believed it, but because it was the only hope I had left. I knew that the first sin God would require an account for would be this lie. Gone were the days of innocence. Life had suddenly become very complicated.

As THE years went by, I kept giving my testimony at every opportunity that came up, hoping that doing so would grow my testimony and make it stronger. It didn't seem to work, but I kept sharing it anyway, desperately craving that one day it would be true. The thoughts of Pharaoh and his predestination continued to plague my thoughts. Why wasn't my testimony getting stronger?

And frankly, the older I got, the more living on the outside of FLDS didn't look so terrible. Howard had left, after all, and God didn't strike him dead. He didn't just leave town; he walked away from everything we had been raised to believe. When Howard left, the family hung their heads, thinking, "Poor Howard; he is so deceived." Howard's choice made him a son of perdition and worthy of the lake of fire. When Howard left, I was thirteen and had been living with my secret of no burning in the bosom for five years.

We considered Howard an apostate, of course, but he would come home periodically. Eventually he attended Utah Tech and became quite a party guy. We were not supposed to associate with him because of his apostasy, but when he showed up on Saturdays to play football with us, no one was there to stop us from playing with our own brother. I remember him coming around in his suped-up silver and black Chevy Camaro. That car was a dream with horses to spare. He took us for rides, and we'd listen to rock 'n' roll music and hear Howard's stories of his new life. He was living wild, but frankly his life didn't seem to be the horde of demons that were supposed to be waiting to devour him once he stepped outside the protective powers of Father's priesthood authority.

Father had always preached diligently against anybody outside our group. On the subject of works versus faith for salvation, he preached about how God was a just God and demanded justice when we fail to keep his laws. If we have done something wrong, God requires that we make right that wrong. Otherwise God is no longer a God of justice. "If God is no longer just," Father argued, "then he would cease to be God!" He went on and on about how to call upon Christ's atonement and then to go on sinning was to deny that atonement. He concluded with how we are saved by grace, through faith, after we have done all that we can do. "This is where born-again Christians err," he proclaimed again and again. He went on and on about the Whore of Babylon and the Great Abominable Church of Satan, otherwise known as Christianity. He made it clear that this was the church of all those who had forsaken the ways of God, including the LDS Mormons who had fallen into apostasy as well.

We were taught that we were predestined to be born into the families we were born into. God had favored us because of our faithful service to him in the pre-existence when there was a great war in heaven. Because we were among the one-third of the hosts that had served God faithfully during the war, we were allowed to come to earth and receive bodies in which to earn our exaltation. We weren't cursed with a black skin like those who didn't fight for God and couldn't decide whom to follow. And we weren't like Satan's demons, who chose to follow him and fight against God and as a result were denied the right to come to earth and receive a body in which they could earn their exaltation. Because we were among the faithful and part of the most valiant defenders of God's kingdom in the pre-existence, God let us be born into families that were already in the faith, thereby assuring us the best possible chance of enduring to the end to attain our own exaltation to godhood.

How could Howard forsake such a pedigree of faith and turn in direct rebellion against what God had done for him?

Yet, without a burning in the bosom, was I any better off?

My first crisis of belief was prolonged and showed no sign of abating as long as I harbored the secret that I had no burning in the bosom. In those years, I didn't know what to do except follow the example set for me by my parents and faithful siblings—and hope that they were right even if I still didn't have a true burning in the bosom several years after my baptism.

9

On Every Side

*Wherefore teach it unto your children, that all
men, everywhere, must repent, or they can in
nowise inherit the kingdom of God, for no unclean
thing can dwell there, or dwell in his presence.*

—*Pearl of Great Price, Moses 6:57*

urning in the bosom or not, daily life in an FLDS community did
not leave a lot of time for children to entertain doubts about the
truth of Mormon teaching. We woke up every morning at about six,
and before we did anything else, the family would gather in the living
room and kneel in a circle to hold hands and pray. Father would ask
someone to pray for the family as a whole, and we also prayed fervently
for the leadership of the FLDS Church, especially Uncle Roy because
he was our Prophet—the president of the Priesthood Council—at that
time. Every day we prayed for God to help us keep a sweet spirit.

That in itself might seem like a worthy prayer, but in our context,
"keep a sweet spirit" was code for submission to leaders and priesthood

heads—anyone with authority over you. Father was my immediate priest-hood head, and if his father had been alive and in the group, he would have been my next immediate priesthood head. Once the line reached the point where a patriarchal father was deceased, the next priesthood head was the lowest ranking Apostle in the Priesthood Council. From there the line of authority moved up the chain to Uncle Roy himself. After that, it would be Joseph Smith, Jesus Christ, and eventually God the Father. To "keep sweet" meant to be obedient and loyal to this line of authority, and we received daily prompts to do so.

Only after this prayer time fraught with fearful reminders of the structures of our faith would the family disperse and carry on with daily activities. We had been duly reminded that our eternal salvation was at stake even before we went out to milk the cows. It was enough to strike fear in the heart of any child who had not truly received a burning in the bosom. I carried my secret with me through all the motions of our religious life together.

The Mormons—both the mainstream LDS Church and the FLDS Church—conduct family home evenings dedicated to the family spending time together learning more about the teachings of the faith while at the same time trying to create closer family bonds. These evenings consist of reading stories aloud, brief performances or demonstrations, and family games. We were encouraged to volunteer to have a part in the family home evening, and sometimes we were appointed to prepare something. Our parents tried to regulate participation so that one child didn't hog all the time and attention. Performing our part could be anything we wanted as long as it was in keeping with the strict codes that governed the behavior in our community. Sometimes we'd act out plays, or perhaps read a poem. The evening generally included some kind of Bible story or *Book of Mormon* story and ended in prayer.

On Sabbath days, we got up and dressed in our Sunday best. Then
we'd head to the living room with our triple combination Scriptures—
Book of Mormon, The Pearl of Great Price, and *Doctrine and Covenants.*
In the living room, the boys would set up the chairs, which were stack-
able and storable, in rows much like you would see in a small church
or in a Sunday school classroom. We even had a podium for Father to
preach from. Father started the proceedings with Sunday school. Every
man had the duty to teach and train his family in the tenets of the
faith, and this was the purpose for this Sunday school session. Father
presided, or perhaps one of the older sons who held an appropriate level
of priesthood.

A boy who has been baptized and confirmed as a member of the
FLDS Church can begin his progression through the two levels of priesthood: first the Aaronic priesthood, and then for some the higher-level
Melchizedek priesthood. At twelve, a boy may be ordained to the office
of deacon in the Aaronic priesthood and begin serving in basic roles in
the church. At fourteen, he may be a teacher, and at sixteen a priest.
The highest level of the Aaronic priesthood is a bishop. The scope of
responsibility increases at each level, even as the number of worthy men
narrows. The Melchizedek priesthood begins with the office of elder
and progresses to high priest, patriarch, Apostle, and Prophet—the one
man who serves as president of the FLDS Church. Obviously fewer
men progress through this higher level of priesthood, but it is important that all men enter the priesthood and begin exercising authority at
some level. Priesthood is required for godhood, though priesthood may
come in the next life.

Whoever was presiding at our family worship would lead us in singing hymns from the LDS Church hymnal while Mother Midge or one
of the girls played the piano. The leader would call on people designated

to read Scripture portions, as well as a predetermined speaker—usually one of the mothers or an older brother—to give a short sermon. Then the grand finale was Father's sermon. Our family service concluded with a hymn.

AT THESE Sunday morning family gatherings, Father systematically preached the essential teaching of the LDS Church about the restoration of true Christianity. The priesthood was restored to the earth through Joseph Smith. However, the FLDS held that the LDS Church's authority was stripped from them because of their apostasy from the founding principles of the Mormon faith. We heard this on a frequent basis on Sunday mornings. We were the true church, the true expression of restored Christianity. Father also emphasized the priesthood authority and the keys of the priesthood for sealing eternal marriages. We heard it so many times. As a boy, it was all I could do to keep from falling asleep! But I knew that falling asleep during a sermon was a sin; it raised questions about your commitment to the faith. If a person with the privilege of being born into the true faith was bored enough to fall asleep, then obviously there was a serious lack of commitment to those in authority.

After our family Sunday school, we would immediately get in the cars and head to Rulon Jeffs's huge house for our Sunday meeting. Many families in the Salt Lake metro area attended the weekly services at Rulon Jeffs's large house in the mouth of Little Cottonwood Canyon near Sandy, Utah. This was a gathering of about seven hundred people, and Rulon Jeffs's house had been constructed to accommodate the entire community. At his house, families split up according to gender and age for appropriate classes.

The women went to a women's class that reinforced a wife's need to submit to her husband as her priesthood head, and emphasized her role in helping him attain godhood by surrendering to his authority and keeping sweet. For wives, "just keep sweet" meant don't rebel, don't speak out, don't defy your husband, and submit to the authority of the priesthood.

Men and older boys who held the priesthood would go off to priesthood meetings corresponding to the level of priesthood they held—the Aaronic or Melchizedek priesthood. The men were instructed in things that were only meant for priesthood members to hear and not the women or children. In the Aaronic priesthood class they discussed the responsibilities of that level of priesthood—how to give the sacrament, home teaching, baptism, leading meetings, preaching, and so on.

Children too young to go to the priesthood meetings went to a Sunday school class for children based on age. Here we learned stories from the *Book of Mormon* or the Bible. Occasionally we read a story about Joseph Smith's youth and the time God and Jesus appeared to him.

My favorite *Book of Mormon* story was the story of Ammon, who went as a missionary to the Lamanites. He is famous for smiting off the arms of the Lamanite thieves who scattered the king's flocks. I loved this story because Mom told me the reason I was named Brian is because it means "strong," and they knew when I was born that God had sent them a child with a strong spirit who could do great things for God. Ammon was strong with the strength that God gave him to fight off thieves, and I wanted to be strong too.

These classes lasted about an hour, then we all went to the meeting room for the main service attended by all the polygamists of our group who lived in the Salt Lake Valley or were visiting from Colorado City. The meeting services were much like what we experienced in our homes. A presiding elder conducted the service, led the singing, called on speakers, and concluded the service. It was a great honor to be called upon to be the presiding elder of the meetings or to be one of the speakers. However, the speakers were usually one of the Priesthood Council members (the Apostles), so the honor was quite limited. Despite their revered status as Apostles, the speakers did not distinguish themselves as orators. The temptation to sleep once again crept in on a regular basis even as I got older, and I thought perhaps if I was predestined as an agent of evil anyway, maybe it wouldn't be such a disaster to nod off. But I could never quite bring myself to take the chance. Quite predictably the speakers droned on reiterating the same central themes we heard from Father at home: submission to priesthood authority, the role of the wives in keeping a sweet spirit in the home, a child's duty to honor parents, the importance of progressing to godhood through priesthood authority. Everything revolved around the hierarchy of worthiness that was at the core of our culture. I kept my mouth shut and didn't tell anyone that I still believed everything only because my parents believed it and not because I knew it to be true for myself.

A wide spectrum of connections resulted from the minglings at Jeffs's house. We all knew which polygamists owned which businesses in town, or where they worked, and who frequented those businesses. If we needed a contractor for work at our own homes, we knew who to call to keep our own people employed. Often these businesses offered a discount to other polygamists. Worshipping together cinched the ties between families regardless of where they lived. It was much more than simply seeing each other in church on Sundays; the community came together because of this shared experience and the reinforced reminder of the authority of the leadership structure.

The families whose children did not attend my father's private school generally attended the school Rulon Jeffs ran in the same facility used for

Sunday meetings. With kids going to school together and families going to church together, community bonds were strong and long-reaching. Growing up, literally no dimension of my life was outside the FLDS culture. Being spread out around the metro area, rather than concentrated in one place, helped us avoid bringing too much attention to ourselves. Other polygamist groups dotted the Salt Lake Valley too. For instance, the Allred group—which my great-uncle Owen Allred led—was located in the southwest corner of the Salt Lake Valley near the Utah State Prison. However, we were not allowed to associate with polygamists from other groups and considered them apostates just as we considered the mainline LDS Church to be apostate. This rule kept me from knowing my own grandparents on my mother's side until I was thirteen years old because they belonged to one of these other groups.

In contrast to groups like ours that tried to blend in and not be noticed, Colorado City was a community of polygamists isolated from the rest of the world. In a sense they drew attention to themselves by separating as much as they did. Sports rivalries sprang up between those who lived in Salt Lake and those who lived at "the Creek" (meaning the Colorado City area, which used to be named Short Creek before the raid of 1953). These rivalries were all in good fun. Sometimes visitors from the Creek would come and play football with us. If there were enough of them we would play the Lakers against the Creekers.

Colorado City had its own school system, police department, fire department, mayor, and every other type of agency you would expect a small town to have—but polygamists ran it all. Every soul who lived in the Creek was a member of the FLDS Church. Take any small town, make them all polygamists, and that's what it looked like to live in Colorado City. However, the men and all the departments of the city answered to the current Prophet. During my childhood, this was Uncle Roy Johnson, then Rulon Jeffs, then more recently his son Warren (who went to prison in 2007 for rape by accomplice for arranging marriages of underage girls to older men.)

Although the structures were not as formalized as in Colorado City, the gatherings at Rulon Jeffs's house yielded a network of relationships that helped us function as one community despite being spread out around the metro area. We were still under the authority of the Prophet, just like the people in Colorado City. No matter where you lived in the Salt Lake Valley, you didn't want to upset the Apostles who made up the Priesthood Council. They were the ones who could influence the president of the FLDS Church, and recriminations were sure to surface when it was time for a man to acquire a new wife or marry his daughter off well. A man who was told he was not worthy to receive a wife from the community had only two choices if he wanted to marry and remain in the community. If he was already married but didn't have the minimum three wives required for godhood, then it fell to him to go out and try to convert a Mormon-minded woman or someone from another polygamist group and romance her. This wasn't an easy task, especially if the woman's parents believed the man to be an apostate because of not being worthy in his own community. The other option was to perform some service for the Priesthood Council that demonstrated the man had renewed his loyalty—but this was no easy feat, either, because there were no fair rules about what would satisfy the council.

ALL OF the land in the FLDS community in Colorado City belongs to a United Effort Plan (UEP) trust. Joseph Smith had tried his own version of communism in the early days of the LDS Church, but it failed because of abuse of the system, and people stopped contributing to the central fund. The FLDS Church has revived the practice, and therefore, all property in Hildale, Utah, and Colorado City, Arizona, was placed into the UEP trust. Those who live in houses in the community live as "tenants at will" and not as homeowners. This means theoretically the leaders could reassign a man and his family to a different home to make room for someone who is more loyal and worthy—or who has a larger family and needs the accommodations the larger house would provide. The UEP is a fearsome entity in the power it exercises over people. Especially in communities like Colorado City, the police department takes its marching orders from the leadership and doesn't dare defy them for fear of recriminations against them personally.

Being displaced from a home generally also means wives are stripped away from their husbands and given to other men. If they remain married to a man who has been determined unworthy, the women will lose their salvation. They cannot progress to godhood unless they are married to a man who holds the priesthood and is on his way to being a god. A man stripped of his priesthood is essentially damned, stopped in his ability to progress toward godhood the way a dam stops the flow of a river. His only hope is to achieve the priesthood in the next life. When a man is prevented from progressing, so are his wives. Their only recourse is to be released from the marriage to this unworthy man and remarry a man who is considered worthy.

Obviously entire families are turned inside out when this happens. The sister wives are not necessarily given to the same man, so half siblings who have grown up together now find themselves not only separated from their fathers, but separated from brothers and sisters and forced to integrate into new households as stepsiblings. If they take on the family name of the new household, keeping track of who is who becomes impossibly complicated. No one wanted to face being stripped away—but it was certainly preferable to damnation!

THE LEADERSHIP of the FLDS Church has its hands in every aspect of the lives of its people. Tracing roots back to the days of Joseph Smith becomes the basis of authority for beliefs and practices that the outside world considers extreme. However, members of the FLDS Church know only that the leaders (Apostles) are the ones who know the truth, the ones who hold the power given by God himself to determine significant decisions in their lives. There is no room for doubt or questioning because even the slightest doubt, if spoken aloud, could lead to unworthiness and thus damnation.

My brother Howard once broached the subject of contradictions within FLDS theology with our father. The answer was, "Put it on the shelf, and wait for God to reveal more to you, and then you will understand." Howard never did get answers to the contradictions he saw. Instead he got only the usual rhetoric about standing firm in spite of the sea of doubts that assailed your mind, followed by the instruction to revisit his testimony that Joseph Smith was a true prophet of God, the *Book of Mormon* was true, and the LDS Church—even though it was currently out of order and in a state of apostasy—was God's one true church that God would eventually set in order.

In the face of doubt, rather than confronting the substantive issues in theological or logical contradictions, we were instructed to go back and revisit that "burning in the bosom" experience, that feeling we had when we knew that we had received our own testimonies—that feeling that I had never experienced for myself. All I could revisit was my chronic anxiety that someone would discover my secret.

When I was eleven and in the throes of my unvoiced perpetual crisis of faith, the crack in the FLDS structure widened. Apostle Richard Jessop died in 1978, and once again Uncle Roy did not replace him with another Apostle. The council was now down to five members—two in favor of the one-man doctrine that would give the Prophet ultimate power with no balances, and three who believed any of the Apostles could receive a revelation. Uncle Roy was now ninety years old and in declining health. Rulon Jeffs, the only other Apostle to espouse the one-man doctrine, lurked in the wings. Our whole lives were surrounded on every side by FLDS doctrine—and Rulon Jeffs intended to keep it that way.

IN THE meantime Mother Maurine left Father. At first she simply moved out of the house, and Father would still go see her. But around the same time Richard Jessop died, Maurine cut Father off completely, understanding that he was never going to leave his other wives for her as he had originally promised. Father's authoritative hold on his own family began to crumble, even as Rulon Jeffs was determined that his grip on the FLDS would never relax.

One of the earliest FLDS gatherings

L to R back row: Joseph Anderson, Isaac Morley, Sidney Rigdon (second president of the LDS Church and advisor to Joseph Smith)
L to R front row: my third great-grandfather, William Moore Allred next to his brothers Reddick Newton and Paulinas Harvey

Lorin C. Woolley, early Mormon fundamentalist leader

Byron Harvey Allred Sr., my
second great-grandfather

William Moore Allred, my third great-grandfather

Clyde Christopher Mackert, my
grandfather on my father's side
(whom I never met)

Byron Harvey Allred Jr., my great-grandfather

Clyde Mackert
My father in his army uniform

Early FLDS leaders
L to R back row: Louis A. Kelsch, Charles F. Zitting
L to R front row: John Y. Barlow, Joseph W. Musser

FLDS Prophet "Uncle Roy" Leroy S. Johnson

L to R: Clyde Mackert, Dan Jessop, Lynn Cooke,
Joseph Barlow, Elmer Johnson, Carl Holm, Louis
Barlow, and Bill Cooke after court appearance

Father's three wives and a few of their children after the 1953 raid on Short Creek, Arizona
L to R back row: Mother Midge, Mother Myra (Mom, pregnant with Rena), and Mother Donna holding Charlotte
L to R front row: Phil, Clyde Jr., Connie, Lucy, Carole, Seth, and Mary

Father's three wives at the time of the 1953 raid
L to R: Mother Donna, Mother Myra (Mom), Mother Midge

Clyde Mackert
Father coming out of the county jail in Kingman, Arizona, after being released on probation following the 1953 raid

Father and his four wives outside the big house in Sandy, Utah
L to R: Mother Donna, Mother Midge, Father, Mother Myra (Mom), Mother Maurine

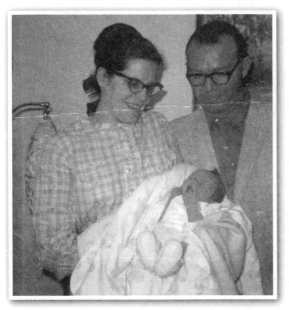

Mom, Father, and me the day I was brought home from the hospital

My half brother and first cousin Mark (left) at four months old and me (right) at thirteen months old

Me at one year old and thirty-three pounds!

Father with thirty of his children and grandchildren at Mother Donna's place in West Jordan, Utah, on Father's Day. I was one year old (I am wearing overalls, pictured in the bottom-right corner of the photo).

All of Father's sons including stepsons (plus Maria) when we moved into the big house in Sandy, Utah
L to R back row: Phil, David, Howard, Clyde Jr., John Swaney (stepbrother) holding Maria, Shem, Seth, Daniel Swaney (stepbrother)
L to R front row: Stan, Steve, me, Ken, Paul with Mark in front of him

My first day of school with my first and only
set of clothes that weren't hand-me-downs

My first-grade school picture

Me on Butch in the front yard after scaring Mom by riding
the horse while standing up

Me at fifteen years old

Me teaching Butch how to jump over a rail

Mom & Sterling (stepfather)

John Swaney (stepbrother), Father, and Rena at John and Rena's wedding

Dana and my wedding photo

10

This Old Guitar

There is no higher authority in matters relating to the family organization, and especially when that organization is presided over by one holding the higher priesthood, than that of the father.... In the home the presiding authority is always vested in the father, and in all home affairs and family matters there is no other authority paramount.

—Joseph F. Smith, "The Rights of Fatherhood," Juvenile Instructor, Mar. 1, 1902, p. 146

I sat in Steve's room and listened to him practice for hours. Steve made the guitar come alive in his hands, as if it was no effort at all. From Steve I learned about the love affair between the musician and the instrument. When I watched him play, I studied every move his fingers made. One night I would devote myself to watching only his left hand, and the next night his right hand. Every note he plucked on those strings thrilled me. I also wanted to impress my brothers, as always. Learning to do something Steve did so well seemed like a perfect way to get his attention and approval.

I worked up the courage to ask Steve to teach me to play. He demonstrated a C chord and told me to keep playing it until I could place all my fingers in the right places and pluck each string without them sounding muted or muffled. He refused to teach me another chord until I could play this one with excellence. The next step was to learn to go back and forth between a G chord and a C chord, with the promise that when I was ready to learn a third chord, I could learn a song. Before I knew it, I was playing a John Denver song that was popular at the time.

And then all I wanted in the world was a guitar of my own. When I told my mother about my desire, her face fell, and so did my heart.

"Your father will never allow it," she said softly.

"But Phil, Steve, and Ken all have guitars," I protested. "Why can they have one and I can't?"

"Because they are Mother Midge and Donna's children and you are mine," she answered.

It was as simple as that. Mom was the third wife, and I was the youngest of her children.

This was the response Mom often gave when I asked for something. There was no point in arguing with her about it. All I could do was try to convince her to make an exception in this case. So every time Mom took me to the secondhand store with her, I would immediately run to find the section of musical instruments. I begged and pleaded whenever I saw a guitar there. Each time my mother's reply was, "Brian, we cannot afford that," or, "Your father won't allow it." It didn't matter that it was only twenty dollars. I had to find a way to make her see that this wasn't impulse buying; it was something I *had* to have. So I started picking up the guitars and playing them while she shopped. I'd let her come and find me when she was done with her shopping. I hoped that perhaps she would hear me playing and realize that this wasn't a passing fancy, but that I was serious about learning to play the guitar and needed one of my own.

One day my mom found an old guitar at a secondhand store; it was a nylon six-string classical that was only ten dollars. She purchased the old guitar as a present for my thirteenth birthday. We never celebrated birthdays with a present or even a cake. The family simply sang "Happy Birthday" during the morning family prayer time, followed by the obligatory thanking of your mother for bringing you into the world. But Mom was getting bolder in the ways she defied Father and brought the guitar home without asking him first. She made me promise not to tell anyone about the guitar, though. I was to keep it hidden, and I was to close my door and only play it when no one was around. If Father discovered I had a guitar, he would take it away.

One more secret to keep.

Now just how often do you think that a house full of people like ours was empty? Never! So I would eat dinner as quickly as I could, and after being excused from the table I would run downstairs to my room and practice. I touched the strings just enough to know I had played the chord correctly, but softly enough that no one outside the room would hear me.

As time went by I got good enough to play new songs and sing along to them. Some songs just aren't meant to be played at a whisper, so one Saturday when Father had gone bowling (his favorite pastime), I let loose and was playing at full throttle. My heart nearly stopped when Father swung my bedroom door open.

What was he doing home?

I sat there, breathless, waiting for Father to speak.

"Where did you get that?" Father snapped.

Everything within me wanted to lie and say it was Steve's guitar and that I had borrowed it, or make up some other excuse to explain the presence of the guitar and keep Father from taking it away from me. But I didn't. "Mom got it for my birthday," I said sheepishly. My birthday had come and gone about two months earlier, which gave Father an indication of how long he had been deceived. I could tell this information only angered him more, and I wished I could have taken the sentence back.

"Give it here," he said, and I handed my beloved guitar to Father, who turned and left my room.

Tears welled in my eyes; I was sure I would never see it again. Father took the guitar up to his study and placed it in his closet. I watched and waited for Mom to come home from work, hoping to warn her about what had happened before she walked in and was blindsided by a confrontation with Father. Amazingly, Father never confronted my mom about why she had gotten me the guitar without his permission or going through the normal procedure of placing it in the study with my name on it for him to give to me if he deemed me worthy of it. Instead Father simply took the guitar and put it in the closet in his study and taped a piece of paper to it with my name on it. Now it was up to me to impress him enough to deserve that guitar.

We would do whatever it took to impress Father. I remember we had an old Chevy pickup truck that threw a rod and the engine had to be replaced. Father bought a junker Oldsmobile with a powerful V8 engine. Paul worked hard to put that engine in the truck so it would be back in commission for all the work on the farm. Some of the other boys also worked on it—handing tools, or helping hold this or that—but Paul did the lion's share of the work. When the engine was replaced and they tried to start it, they had some difficulty, which is not surprising with an old engine that hasn't run in a while. Howard happened to come up about then and made a few adjustments, and the engine cranked over. He then walked into the house and told Father he was finished changing out the engine in the truck and it was running fine. Howard took all the credit for Paul's hard work. Impressing Father was even worth betraying a brother.

Growing up, I had managed to view enough forbidden TV shows and old movies to know that fathers loved their sons, were proud of their sons, helped their sons achieve their goals. I watched *Bonanza* and saw a father living and working with his sons. I saw how the Brady Bunch worked out their blended-family issues. I saw the wise concern of the father on *Eight Is Enough*. If this was the norm, why was it that my own father hardly even acknowledged my existence unless I was in some sort of trouble? When Father came home from work at the end of the day, I would be paralyzed with fear that if I so much as moved the wrong way I would get into trouble. It was like walking on broken glass waiting for the next disciplinary session with him.

I fantasized that somewhere out there I had a *real* father. I was even willing to suppose that my mother had been unfaithful so I could be another man's son. I would imagine that for whatever reason, he didn't know of my existence. But soon he would find out about me, and I would have a father who loved me, who wanted to spend time with me, who was proud of me, who accepted me, and who could even forgive my shortcomings.

I decided the only way that I could get Father to give me the guitar was to make sure that all he ever heard about me was good. So I worked extra hard to stay out of trouble: I never talked back, I obeyed all of my elders, completed all my chores, and even went the extra mile by assisting in other areas without being asked. Father had on occasion asked me to shine his shoes for him, so I went into Father's room and got all of his shoes out of his closet and made sure that all of them were freshly polished. I made sure that every night the shoes Father had worn that day got a touch-up of polish so that in the morning he could choose from any of the shoes in his closet and have a freshly shined pair.

After about a month of this good behavior, I became discouraged. I kept checking the closet to see if the guitar was still there and if it still had my name on it. Another month passed as I waited for Father to recognize my repentant deeds. The waiting was more than I could bear. One day while I was watching Steve, he finished playing and I let out an audible sigh.

"What's wrong?" he asked.

"It's Father. He still has my guitar. I have been good for so long now; how long does Father expect me to keep this up?" I asked. "I think he just wants to torture me."

"Have you thought about giving Father a really good reason to give you the guitar?" Steve asked.

"Haven't you heard a thing I've said? I have been showing him a repentant heart for two months now." Maybe he hadn't even noticed; he generally didn't anyway.

"You still haven't given him the best reason of all," Steve said. "Play the guitar for him; play a song on the guitar the next time you have a part to perform in family home evening, and Father will see that giving you a guitar is the right thing to do."

It was sheer brilliance. In that single moment Steve became the smartest person on the face of the earth in my estimation.

"I'll need a guitar to play on," I said longingly.

"You can use mine," he offered. The right answer!

While I awaited my turn to perform in our family home evening,

I practiced as often as I could. At first I chose a difficult song, thinking that the more difficult it was the better my chances would be of pleasing Father. But my nerves got the best of me. In the end I chose a simple song with a well-known melody. I remembered listening to my sisters practicing at the piano and thinking that their playing was very good because they could play something I recognized. My strategy was that playing a song Father recognized would impress him.

The real brilliance of Steve's plan was that Father was a musician too; he played the violin. I remember the excitement that would overcome the whole family whenever Father surprised us with a rare performance during a family home evening. Under Father's dancing fingers, the violin expressed the full spectrum of emotion from violent rage to overwhelming joy to the depth of depression to the sensual caress of a lover. I loved to listen to him play with my eyes closed. Steve had given me a scheme that played to Father's weakness and in all likelihood would sway him in favor of giving me the guitar.

Finally my performance date came. I was nervous as I set up my chair and music stand, so nervous that my announcement of the song's title was barely audible. I picked up the guitar and after murdering the introduction during three attempts, I managed to get the song started off right. I fumbled my way through the first verse and chorus, and showed no mercy to the second verse. Then, not wanting to prolong the suffering, I quickened the tempo and killed it dead by galloping through the chorus. Embarrassed by my complete failure in my mission, I listened as Steve and Ken assured me that I had done all right. I wanted to die! I had won the sympathy vote from the audience, but what Father thought is what counted. I felt like one of those disappointed figure skaters in the Olympics who, after falling down, has to wait for the judges' reactions to the performance. No matter how the crowd responds, what matters is the scores the judges give. Those who knew my scheme were all giving me reassurances I had done all right, but I knew it was a disaster.

"Brian, Father wants to see you in his study," I heard someone say a bit later.

My heart sank! If only I had won the sympathy vote from Father all would be well. I walked into the study. "You wanted to see me, Father?"

Father walked over to the closet and opened the door, leaned inside and withdrew from it with the guitar. He turned the tag to read the name on it as if to ensure he was giving the guitar to the rightful recipient. "It's obvious to me that you'll need this," he said as he held out the instrument to me.

"Thank you, Father," I said, taking the guitar from him gingerly.

"You played well tonight," he said. "Keep practicing and you'll make a fine musician."

"Yes, sir," I said as I turned and walked out of his study. I grinned like the cat that swallowed the canary. It was the kindest thing I ever remember Father saying to me about anything that I had ever done. It's sad to think about it now, but it is the only approval I remember receiving from Father as a young boy.

I showed my reclaimed prize to all and then headed downstairs to my room where I played it until I was commanded to put it away and go to bed before Father changed his mind. Sleep didn't come easy that night as I replayed my performance in my head. I died a thousand deaths of embarrassment as I stared at the ceiling and recalled every mistake.

As I drifted off to sleep, the songs of artists like John Denver; Jim Croce; James Taylor; Simon & Garfunkel; Peter, Paul & Mary; and other greats of folk music of the time played in my head. I dreamed it was me playing on my guitar and that my fingers were hammering, pulling, bending, and plucking at the strings, making the beautiful music that filled my head.

Suddenly I bolted upright in bed. Anxiously I peered at the closet through the darkness. A sigh of relief escaped my lips when I finally glimpsed the old guitar sitting in the corner of the closet just where I had left it. It wasn't a dream; it was real. The old guitar was mine.

11

All Is Well in Zion

*And others will he pacify, and lull them away into carnal
security, that they will say: All is well in Zion; yea, Zion
prospereth, all is well—and thus the devil cheateth their
souls, and leadeth them away carefully down to hell.*

—Book of Mormon, 2 Nephi 28:21

"Airman Mackert, the doctor will see you now," the receptionist
announced.

I got up and walked the familiar steps to his office for my third visit.
Our conversations had stirred up so many memories that I was relieved
to be somewhere I could dump them out and perhaps put them back
together in a way that made some sense.

"Well, Brian," the doctor said after opening pleasantries, "we've
covered a lot about your family, but we haven't discussed how the mothers got along. Can you tell me about that?"

"It wasn't always the happy family we projected," I admitted. "Yes,
we loved each other. Yes, we cared for each other. But there were rivalries

between us, between mothers and their children. It went beyond a fight for resources to take care of children. It was also a struggle for the love, affection, and attention of Father," I said. "Mother Midge was Father's first wife and the only one he married because he loved her—with the possible exception of Mother Maurine, whom Father met in a bar."

"Your Father frequented bars in spite of his religious beliefs?" he asked, surprised.

"Oh yeah, Father was a hypocrite when it came to smoking, drinking, and visiting local bars," I informed him. "Father promised Maurine he would leave all his wives and run away with her."

"Did he follow through?" he asked.

"No. In fact she ended up leaving him because he would never make good on that promise. Father only wanted to add her to his harem," I said. "Naturally all the mothers resented her and her four children."

"So there was some sort of hierarchy among the wives?"

I nodded. "Mother Midge was the top dog when it came to Father's wives. Her children got things the rest of us could only dream about. Mother Maurine was second in his affections, but not in authority," I told him.

"What do you mean by 'not in authority'?"

I had to remind myself I was speaking to someone outside the FLDS system. I couldn't just use the old lingo and expect him to get it, but I hoped I wouldn't have to spend all of my time teaching him to speak "polyg."

"Mother Maurine pretty much did what she wanted," I explained. "She was a convert who never really tried to be a good fundamentalist. Being with my father was the only reason she came. Father didn't ask permission from the Priesthood Council; he just brought her into the house because he wanted her. She couldn't possibly understand the intricacies of the pecking order, so she just stayed out of it, like she was above it all. Mother Donna was the dominant one who was really in charge, even though she was the second wife."

"What about your mother?" he asked.

"Mom was the peacemaker. She tried to live in peace with all Father's wives, so she hardly ever fought for a fair share of the available resources. Mom was more concerned with trying to be the best wife she could be and live in harmony with the rest of the family, and that meant not sticking up for herself or her children. Don't get me wrong, my mother wasn't a saint, but that's the excuse she always gave me for why she didn't defend us or stand up for us."

"What was your relationship like with your siblings?" the doctor asked. "Were children treated differently based on who the mother was?"

I nodded. "Many of my siblings, mostly those who weren't my mother's children, deny the favoritism and pecking order," I explained. "It's hard to recognize injustice when it's not aimed at you. But it really did happen, and it had a trickle-down effect on the children. If your mother was at the top of the pecking order, you knew you were superior somehow, and you projected that superiority onto your subordinate siblings.

"Mother Midge's kids picked on everyone and got away with more stuff. Mother Donna was the second wife, so her kids picked on Maurine's kids and my mother's kids. But Maurine's kids were a lot older and could stick up for themselves. The youngest were always at the bottom of the pecking order, so being my mom's youngest meant the pecking order stopped with me. I could try to pick on my younger sisters, but my position was usually trumped by their status as Mother Donna's children."

"You didn't have any older siblings from your mother's family who would stand up for you?" he asked.

"Well, Paul, for a while, but then Paul ran away from home because of his problems with Father," I said. "Laura stood up for me a couple of times with Mother Donna, but she got such a raw deal that I started being an awful brother to her so she would stop defending me. I didn't want her taking any more of Mother Donna's rage on my behalf, so I was a rebellious little hellion to the point that Laura would hate me and stop defending me."

"What on earth happened to Laura that you felt you had to go to such extremes?" the doctor inquired.

"Mother Donna broke a broom handle over her back once when Laura defended me," I said. "We were all having a water fight in the house. But when Mother Donna caught us, she singled me out to punish and was letting her own children off scot-free. Laura felt the need to correct the injustice and started yelling at Mother Donna. I watched in horror as Laura got what should have been my punishment to the tenth power. From that day on I didn't want Laura defending me anymore. I thought it was better to take any punishment Mother Donna dished out, whether it was just or unjust, simply to spare anyone who might get in the way."

"Were beatings like this isolated incidents?" he asked.

"No." It was the plain truth. While I didn't remember anything more severe than a belt strap at the hands of my father, Mother Donna was another question, and she was the one who was always home.

"How did all of this make you feel?" he asked. "It sounds like you felt the world was ganging up on you."

"I hated it! Because I was the youngest of my mother's children, everything came crashing down on me," I said. "It wasn't fair! I just wanted out of there. When I was seven, it got to the point that I couldn't take it anymore. So I made my plans to run away from home."

"At the age of seven!" he said in astonishment. "Things were that bad that you were going to run away from home when you were only seven?"

"Yeah, I know," I said.

"Did you run away?" he asked.

"No."

"What stopped you?"

"My sister Maria."

The whole story spilled out. I told him about how I went down to my bedroom and took the blanket off my bed and snuck it outside to the hiding place Mark and I had behind the old tree stump in the corner of the backyard. Then I returned to the house and began stealing provisions from the cellar. I made many trips, sometimes carrying only one item at a time to keep from looking suspicious. I put items in the blanket and covered it with leaves.

When I felt I had enough, I collected my coat, boots, gloves, and a few changes of clothes. I intended to go down to the State Street bridge about a mile from the house and live there. When the food ran out, I figured I would sneak back into the house at night and raid the cellar again. I hoped God would help me find a new family or a new way of providing for myself eventually.

I was just about to throw my blanket over my shoulder and head for the tree line, where I wouldn't be seen until I got to the bridge, when I heard the back door slam. Four-year-old Maria was charging me. So much for the hiding place. She came behind the tree and said she had been watching me from the window and saw I was hiding food out there and she demanded to know what it was for.

When Maria realized I was running away, she burst into tears. She avowed she was going to follow me to make sure I was all right. If I was leaving, she was leaving too! I told her I couldn't take her with me, and if she tried to follow me I would just ditch her like Mark and I had always done when we didn't want her tagging along. Maria began weeping uncontrollably, begging me not to go, and telling me she loved me. I looked into the eyes of my little sister and my determination cracked. As Mother Donna's child, she was one of the people I considered an enemy to me in our house, and here she was begging me not to go, crying, and pouring her heart out. How could I possibly go? If there was one person in the family who loved me that much, maybe I could endure the rest.

So Maria joyfully helped me carry the blanket full of food and clothes back into the house and unpack it. She made sure that we got it all put back so no one would know the difference. It was our little secret.

"WELL, THAT story sure makes it clear to me how far a little expression of love goes for you," the doctor said. "I think I've got the picture about how things were at home. Now explain to me your mother's relationship with your father."

I started with the facts, though that was not really what he asked.

"Well, Mom married Father when she was nineteen. Father already had Mother Midge and Mother Donna as wives at the time," I said. According to Mom, Father approached my grandfather wanting to marry my mother first. My grandfather didn't like my father, but the Priesthood Council prevailed. However, Apostle Guy Musser said that my mother couldn't be married until her older sister was married first. So Father married Mother Donna and then came back and asked for my mom the next year.

"And Mother Donna and your mom didn't have a problem being married to the same man?" he asked. He wasn't going to settle for the facts, was he? He was determined to get to the emotions whether I wanted to go there or not.

"Well, publicly they will tell you that they didn't, but privately they have always had squabbles between them about one thing or another. Mom, I suppose, always resented the fact that Mother Donna continued her domineering role as the older sibling even after they were married. The best way that I can describe it would be a sibling rivalry that was complicated by the fact that they were now sister-wives. Mom has always resented the way Donna would run over her."

"Okay, I think I understand the underlying conflict between Donna and your mother. Let's get back to your mother's relationship with your father," he suggested.

I had the sense that the doctor was looking for something in particular, and I wasn't sure I wanted to go there. I went into analysis mode instead. I could talk about this if I detached myself enough. What did the relationship between my parents have to do with anything, anyway? I was here because I wanted to kill my father. I was still thinking about that, planning when and how, but instead of focusing on that, the psychiatrist was delving around my parents' marriage. At least he wasn't asking about the real issue yet.

"Well, Mom always believed that of all of Father's wives, she pleased him the most because she tried not to be a source of friction. Mom told me that Father always complimented her on how peaceful it was when he was with her, complimented her on her ability to please him sexually, and stuff like that. But can you really trust statements like that?"

"What do you mean?" the doctor asked.

"Well, think about it from Father's perspective," I suggested, logic ramping up. "If you were married to four women and you wanted to keep each one happy in spite of the fact that you had three other wives, how would you go about accomplishing that? One way would be to make sure each one felt special in some way, that she had a place in your heart reserved for her alone."

"I see what you mean," he acknowledged. "Do you believe your father was lying to your mother?"

"I don't know," I replied. "There is no way for me to know. I suppose at some level my mother brought something unique into their relationship, but I find it easier to believe my father said the same kinds of things to all his wives. I know how gullible my mother is and how easily she gives her heart away and refuses to see the obvious in order to make the worst situations look rosy."

"Why do you say that your mother is gullible?" he asked.

"I've seen the way she is," I said. "She refuses to see the truth in a situation regardless of how much evidence there is. She revises reality to make it fit what she wants it to be."

"So you don't believe that your mother was capable of dealing with reality but created her own sense of reality?" he asked.

"Exactly!" I exclaimed. "It fits what was modeled for us. We weren't allowed to let on there were problems in our home. We weren't allowed to be human. First there was the perception of the outside world. Whatever image we projected had to communicate that we were God's people. We had to bear fruit in keeping with that title. We dressed differently, we acted differently, we loved one another, and there was harmony in the home—or at least that was the image we were supposed to project. If you were a man, you had to demonstrate you were worthy of the wives you had and worthy of additional wives as well. The motto was 'All is well in Zion,' regardless of how bad things were. This was the only life my mother ever knew. Remember, her family had been polygamous for six generations. The training she received as a child taught her to deny reality and see things as she wants to see them, rather than for what they are."

I was well aware at that moment that I was of the same lineage. As the seventh generation, I had absorbed the same culture—subjugate your emotions at all cost. Fear of damnation trumped anything we felt.

Only now I wanted to kill my father, and I wasn't suppressing that.

"I see; you feel this is a conditioned response to reality," the doctor summarized.

"Absolutely!"

"Okay, let's get back to your mother's relationship with your father," he prompted me again. "Did they love each other?"

Never once had I seen a display of affection between my parents. Never once. Whatever Father felt for any of his wives, he kept to himself.

"I know she loved him," I began. "I don't know that he loved her, though. When they got divorced I comforted her when she cried, tried to be strong for her, and helped her sort out the emotions she went through as a result of the divorce. I wasn't around to see how it affected my father. When we moved out, I went with my mom and never once had a conversation with my father about the divorce."

"Well, that leads me to my next question," he said. "Talk to me about the circumstances surrounding your parents' divorce."

Here we were at last, getting into the real issues I didn't feel like talking about, but had to—or I might really kill my father. Where would I begin? The memories came flooding back faster than I could put them into words.

WHEN I was thirteen, Mom started squirreling things away after school had let out for the summer. During the summertime we would stack all the school furniture in one room of the school. This freed up rooms to be used as bedrooms for the summer, which relieved the congestion for those who were doubled up during the school year. Mom made me go with her and rearrange all the desks and chairs so there was a space behind them not visible from the front of the room. This is where she stashed her loot. She would scrimp and save all that she could whenever she went grocery shopping and use what she saved to purchase the things she needed. At first she told me she was storing up things for when Laura got married. As the pile grew too large for that explanation, Mom said that it never hurt to have extra things for the house on hand. She would go shopping at the thrift stores and bring home items she got a good deal on—dishes, pots, pans, silverware, towels, sheets, and blankets. This went on for months. I thought she had lost her mind. It never occurred to me she was preparing to make her getaway. After all, my mother had had a real burning in the bosom, so her sixth-generation faith was true.

When the time came, Mom came to me and told me that she was leaving Father. She couldn't bear the thought of leaving me behind and wanted me to leave with her. I didn't have to give it any thought. I gave her my answer before she could even start explaining the plans she had for where we would go and how we would get by without the rest of the family. All I knew was I wanted out too. I had wanted out since I was seven, and I was thirteen now. It didn't matter where we were going or what we were doing as long as we were leaving the farm and going someplace new.

Mom told me that we were going to go live with Grandma a few miles to the south in Draper, Utah. The whole reason she had been storing up things in the basement was to prepare for this day, so that when she left, she had more than the clothes on her back to help establish a new life for us. I wanted to go, but suddenly it struck me—why did Mom? After all these years, why did she want to leave Father? Mom sat me down to say something that couldn't have been easy for her.

"Brian, your father has done some things that I just cannot live with," she said. "He has done some very bad things that cannot be forgiven or made right." I stared at her, puzzled by the look in her eyes that I couldn't quite interpret. Was it sadness? Hurt? Disgust? I'd never seen my mother look quite like this, and I was frightened. Mother took a long, agonizing breath before letting out the words I will never forget. "Your father has been molesting your sisters."

Molesting my sisters? *My father was molesting my sisters?* I didn't even know what questions to ask.

Mom laid out her case—what my sister Rena had told her and the things she had seen and heard for herself over time. I went into a trance, as if I were dreaming and at any moment I would wake up and it wouldn't be real. But it was real. Instantly some of the icky feelings I had known over the years made sense. I had been too young and naive to know what the signs meant, but looking back I know I had seen some of them for myself.

I recall a time when I saw my father sexually aroused after my then six-year-old sister, Melanie, sat in his lap for most of an evening. At the time I didn't make the connection between what I observed and what he might be feeling about the little girl—his own daughter.

And what about all the times Kathy had hidden under the table?

And the fear in my sisters' eyes every day when Father came home from work. They were petrified—but why? I had never known.

I couldn't help but notice the way Father's glance often lingered after my sisters—or the way he sometimes grazed a hand across them.

What about his insistence that the girls stay close to the house, while the boys were freer to leave the property? Or the story that he had once lined up his older daughters to perform breast exams to make sure they were developing properly?

A light snapped on. Instantly I believed what Mom said. Mary, Rena, Kathleen, Laura—all of them! And how many of my half sisters? It had been going on for years, one daughter after another. They were helpless to protect each other, helpless to defy the priesthood authority, helpless to have any control over their own lives.

My heart chilled! How could he? This was the man who raised me to honor and revere women because they bring life into this world. He taught me to respect them and protect them. I was supposed to be willing to lay down my life to defend a woman I didn't even know; even if she was a prostitute, I was supposed to be willing to give my life in her defense. The man who taught me and my brothers this code of honor had turned out to be the very man from whom my sisters needed protection. Had I failed them somehow by not recognizing the signs?

I wanted to vomit.

"BRIAN, ARE you all right?"

The doctor's question jarred me back to the moment. "Fine," I said.

"I thought I'd lost you there for a moment," he said. "Why did your parents get divorced?"

My eyes filled with tears. I had yet to speak aloud the words that carried the reason for my presence in this office. Swallowing hard, I tried to look the psychiatrist in the eyes when I said it, but I couldn't; I was too ashamed. I looked to the window and found no escape there.

I looked behind me at the door and thought of just getting up and leaving. Against my will, I started to cry.

"Brian, is this too hard a question for you to answer right now?" he asked.

I looked up at him with tears streaming down my face now. "Yes!" I shouted. I could not speak the terrible secret aloud. The tears came undammed as I buried my face in my hands. My sobs exploded until there were no more tears left and all that remained was the aching in the back of my throat from the painful moans of my crying.

The weight of the doctor's hand on my shoulder made me gasp. Over the years I had ached for my father to touch me with compassion, to show me I mattered. But he didn't. This man I barely knew—and who still did not know the unspeakable secret—touched me in my despair.

With his other hand he offered a tissue. I took it and dried my eyes. He immediately reached for another and held it, waiting for when I would want that one, too. I took it and blew my nose.

I looked up at him. "I knew this was going to happen!" I said. "I knew eventually we would get to this point! It's the reason I didn't want to come here in the first place!"

"Why did you come here, then?" he asked.

"Because I hate my father so much I want to kill him!" I sobbed.

"Is the reason that you want to kill your father—because he divorced your mother and abandoned you?" he asked.

"No," I said, "it isn't that." I took a deep breath and looked down at my shoes again. I knew I had to get the words out in order for my healing to begin. "My father ... my father molested my sisters," I stammered as the tears began to flow again.

"Oh, my!" he said, with unrestrained surprise. "So your mother discovered what he was doing and left him?"

"Yeah, that's it," I said.

"Were you the only child still at home when your mother left?" he asked.

"Yes. My sister Laura, the last of the girls, was seventeen at the time, and she was living with my brother Shem and his wife who just had twins."

"So there isn't anyone left at home who still might be in any danger of your father's pedophilia?" he asked.

"No," I said. "Mother Donna is the only one who has children younger than me and she left Father as well, so right now it's just Father and Mother Midge living together; everyone else has left."

"How did the rest of the family respond to this revelation?" he asked.

"Well, only my mother's daughters confessed that they had been molested," I said, "so much of the family didn't believe them and said it was all a lie."

"Well, obviously Mother Donna believed them or she wouldn't have left too, right?" he asked.

"Yeah, that's right," I said.

"So this has divided the family?"

"You could say that."

"Are you okay?"

I couldn't believe he asked that. "I'm having a meltdown here! How do you *think* I'm doing?"

He clarified. "What I mean is, you've managed to survive up to this point with the knowledge of your father's abuse. Are you going to be okay, or do you need some medication to help you cope?" he asked.

"No, I don't need any meds—just some time to pull myself together," I replied.

"Okay, when you come in next week, we'll discuss this further," he assured me. "Until then I want you to relax and try not to dwell too much on it. Just make sure that if you feel like you're going to hurt yourself or anyone else you call here first and get the help you need to make it through. Okay?"

"No problem, Doc," I said. "I didn't come this far to do something stupid. I'll see you next week."

As I left the hospital and headed back to my squadron at Miramar Naval Air Station, the cool ocean breeze was almost as refreshing as my session had been. I had never dreamed that speaking the truth could be so freeing. It felt good to finally get it off my chest; it felt good to be able to talk to someone. But most of all it felt good to cry about it for a change instead of keeping it all in. Whether or not I was making progress, one thing was certain: Things were somehow different. I wanted to get it all out and deal with it once and for all. I wanted to be free of it. For the first time in a long time—perhaps for the first time in my life—I had hope.

12

Beyond Sandy

But when we undertake to cover our sins ... or to exercise
control or dominion or compulsion upon the souls of
the children of men, in any degree of unrighteousness,
behold the heavens withdraw themselves; the Spirit of
the Lord is grieved; and when it is withdrawn, Amen
to the priesthood or to the authority of that man.

—Doctrine and Covenants, Section 121:37

The week had blown by with amazing speed, and I found myself once again in the office of my shrink. He offered me a seat and already had a bottle of water and a glass waiting for me.

"How have you been doing since our last session?" he inquired. "We broke into some pretty deep stuff; how has it affected you?"

"Actually, it was like having the weight of the world lifted off my shoulders," I said.

"Good!" he exclaimed. "Last week you told me about your father's sexual abuse of your sisters and that it was the reason behind your parents' divorce. Tell me what happened after your mother revealed this to you."

I poured myself my usual water as I remembered how eager I was to leave with my mother. Then I plunged in to tell the story.

The breakup of my family, and the tumultuous years that followed in my life, coincided chronologically with the fragmenting of the authority structure of the FLDS Church. By 1980, the year my mother left my father, Uncle Roy was ninety-two years old and clearly had no intention of replacing the Apostles who had preceded him in death. In 1983, Apostle Guy Messer died, leaving the council evenly split on the one-man doctrine issue: Uncle Roy and Rulon Jeffs affirmed it; Marion Hammon and Alma Timpson did not. Rulon's dilemma was that Marion Hammon was the next senior Apostle to Uncle Roy. If Uncle Roy were to die, the mantle would fall to the side that believed all the Apostles could receive revelations, and Marion would no doubt begin appointing new Apostles. What Rulon Jeffs had on his side, however, was his control of the United Effort Plan trust that united the finances of the polygamist families in Colorado City. He literally had the power to kick out anyone who didn't see things his way. Even though he was not the senior Apostle, he already wielded great power. Rulon also carried the blessing of Uncle Roy because they agreed on the one-man doctrine. Members of the community who rode the fence about the doctrine itself would likely follow Rulon out of respect and loyalty to Uncle Roy.

Because my parents' marriage wasn't a legal marriage, but a "spiritual" one, it didn't require a legal divorce. Two members of the Priesthood Council, Marion Hammon and Alma Timpson, gave my mother what they called a "release," which dissolved a marriage covenant that was supposed to be sealed for time and all eternity. She agreed with their belief on the one-man doctrine.

My father had surprised all of us by declaring loyalty to the other side of the question. For years Father had taught us that God can give revelation to whomever he pleases; he is not bound to speak only to the Prophet. When my sister Camille was seventeen, while the debate still rumbled through the Priesthood Council, she was taken to Uncle Roy's house to be married to the man the leaders had selected for her, and Father had his thumbs twisted. After the ceremony, Uncle Roy grilled Father on his position and finally asked him point blank whose side he was on.

"Your side, of course," Father said. To everyone's amazement, he had buckled under pressure.

Because of his loyalty, Uncle Roy and Rulon later offered a safe harbor for my father when accusations about incest began to fly. Marion and Alma naturally provided a wall around my mother, who had never wavered in her own conviction about revelations. My family drifted along both sides of the fence.

This climate of taking up sides before Uncle Roy's death was the perfect context for Mom to execute the escape she had dreamed of for several years. Having acquired her release, Mom was now free from Father and didn't have to be concerned about spending an eternity married to a child molester. She was free to marry another man who could take her into the Mormon celestial kingdom.

MOM HAD arranged for us to go and live with her mother, Grandma Rhea. Growing up, I hardly knew Grandma, although she lived nearby. Father was such a control freak that we weren't allowed to visit her. My grandparents had divorced a long time ago, but both were firm believers in the fundamental teachings of the Mormon faith. Even though they were fundamentalist Mormons, we weren't allowed to associate with them. Father's reasoning was that they didn't belong to our particular polygamist group, so therefore they would be a bad influence on us. I was Grandpa's one hundredth grandchild, but because of Father's interference, his family didn't even know I had been born. They had planned a big celebration for Grandpa's one hundredth grandchild, and they threw their party for my cousin when she was born instead of having it for me.

Grandma came from a long line of polygamist Mormons who played vital roles in the early practice of plural marriage and establishing its essential part in our path to godhood. She would wax strong and long about all the things she had seen, heard, and knew to be true that confirmed not only the truth of Mormonism, but that the LDS Church as it stood today was in an apostate condition and needed to be restored by the "One Mighty and Strong" who was prophesied to come and restore all things. I loved sitting and listening to Grandma's stories of what life was like as a girl. She grew up without automobiles or electricity, had lived through two world wars, and raised a family during the Great Depression. Grandma Rhea was the very definition of Mormon pioneer stock if ever there was one.

I didn't know my grandparents on Father's side, either. Father was disowned by his family when they discovered he was a polygamist. They weren't aware of Father's lifestyle until *LIFE Magazine* featured my family in an article about the 1953 raid on Short Creek, Arizona. When my grandfather discovered his son had become a polygamist, he disowned him. Father didn't have any contact with them after that. Because Father forbid us to visit with my grandparents on Mom's side of the family, essentially the only family I knew was Father's immediate family, and now we were separating from them.

Mom had thought about this transition from my point of view. I remember Mom taking me over to Grandma's when the family thought she was out shopping. She always made me promise not to tell anyone we were at Grandma's. It was just another secret in a long line of secrets—no big deal. The same was true of Grandpa Morris. Mom knew I would be lonely without my siblings and wanted to make the change easier by introducing me to my extended family.

GRANDMA HAD a large house in Draper, Utah, that had been divided up into three different apartments. She lived in about one-third of the first and second floors. A winding staircase went from her living room to the upstairs areas of her apartment. My aunt Karen lived in the rest of the upstairs area, and Mom and I moved into the remainder of the bottom floor. Mom thought this was an ideal situation. She traveled a lot in her job, and with Grandma, Aunt Karen, and two of my cousins there, I wouldn't be lonely and would have the supervision I needed.

I had not yet completed the eighth grade, so Mom made sure I finished it at Father's private school. That helped in making the transition; I was able to see my siblings when I went over for school. After school hours, I stayed there with Mother Donna and hung out with Mark and Ken while I waited for Mom to pick me up.

After I completed the eighth grade, I started correspondence courses to finish my high school education. However, I found correspondence school boring and didn't have the drive to learn from a book without the help of a teacher. I stopped doing my schoolwork and dropped out completely. No one seemed to notice anyway; it wasn't so unusual in FLDS circles. When I turned fourteen, Mom sent me to stay with my brother Shem in Cedar City, in the southern end of the state, so

I could learn the trade of carpentry. She also felt that it would do me good to have a male role model in my life. I wondered how she could have thought Father was ever a male role model for me. Why did she suddenly think it was so important to give me something I'd never had before? Still, it was nice to be around Shem and his family. Shem didn't attend any polygamist meetings but claimed to still believe. Ken was there as well, though he had apostatized and had no religion.

I loved working with Shem; he knew how to motivate me to work hard and fast all day long to get as much work done as possible. I learned my work ethics from growing up on a farm and from Shem. He also spent some of his spare time with me, something Father certainly had never done. We'd go rabbit hunting and fishing on the way to and from work. I had never done these things before and loved the outdoor excursions with my brother. After awhile, Mother Donna sent Mark down too, so Mark and I were together again working for Shem. With Ken and Mark there, it was like my family core had simply relocated to Cedar City. I still had my brothers—but didn't have to see the fear in my siblings' eyes when Father walked into the room.

Work dried up in Cedar City, and we had worn out our welcome at Shem's. It was time for me to go home and stay with Mom again after being with Shem for almost a year. Now I started working with my oldest brother, Clyde Jr., and continued to learn the carpentry trade.

WHEN I was fifteen, my mom remarried to a man named Wayne Horsley. Wayne was one of the members of our polygamist group, and his daughters Julie and Susan married my brothers Clyde Jr. and Seth. He lived in Cedar City with his first two wives; my mother continued to live in Salt Lake City, and Wayne would visit. Three of Wayne's sons often came out to play football, tennis, or softball with us, so I knew them already. I understood that Mom had to remarry for the sake of her salvation, and it was nice to know it was someone whose sons I was already friends with. I had fantasized all my life about having a real father; I hoped Wayne wanted another son as much as I wanted a father.

Wayne's son Paul and I became peas in a pod, though not very good Mormons. Paul introduced me to heavy metal and punk rock music. We would sneak out at night and go to the teenage dance halls. I started hanging out with the bad kids in the neighborhood, learned to smoke—including pot—and started partying. It wasn't hard to get someone to buy us beer on the weekends.

Wayne asked me to come down to Cedar City and work for him for a while. This was my chance! I could be close to my new father. I even considered changing my last name to Horsley as a gesture to encourage him to accept me. I tried really hard to be a good son to him, but I had already developed some destructive habits hanging around with Paul. While vowing to show respect, I continued to party as much as I could. I never would have had the emotional fortitude to understand it at the time, but I was coming apart at the seams on the inside. I had to stay on the straight and narrow to progress to godhood, and Wayne could help me. Maybe that burning in the bosom would still come. But I also wanted to pummel my fists at the deceit and hypocrisy that had been the story of my life. I wanted a real father, but I also wanted to duke it out with the universe because I was so angry at my own father.

Irene, Wayne's first wife, was about the same age as Mom and was the mother of all the Horsley boys. Wayne's second wife was a sixteen-year-old girl who was the daughter of Apostle Marion Hammon. Wayne became quite infatuated with his young bride and spent most of his time with her at the expense of my mom. Because both Irene and Wayne's second wife lived together in the same house, Irene didn't have to go long without Wayne's presence; she only had to deal with the competition of having a sixteen-year-old sister-wife. However, Wayne's visits to Mom in Salt Lake City became more and more infrequent. Mom would go for months at a time without seeing him. Then Wayne moved both of his other wives from Cedar City to Salt Lake City, while he was still working in Cedar City. Wayne would come into town and rush over to his other house to see his young bride and wouldn't even let Mom know he was in town. This was not the father I had imagined when Wayne and Mom got married. He was just more deceit and hypocrisy.

By this time Wayne was really getting on my nerves. It was as if he were ashamed of my mother and had only married her to complete the religious requirement of having three plural wives in order to progress to godhood. And he had no use for me. I was nothing more than a reminder that my mother had been with another man. My worthlessness to a father was something I knew well, but this time I had more choice. I didn't want to work for Wayne anymore, so I quit. I moved back home with Mom and started working with Clyde Jr. again.

My search for a father at a dead end, Paul Horsley and I continued to party every weekend. We snuck away on weeknights to visit the local teenage discos. The first Ozzy Osbourne song I ever heard was from an album Paul owned. During this time, Mother Donna left Father and moved in with Grandma Rhea, bringing Mark with her, so Paul and I tried to suck him into our rebellion. We convinced Mark to dress up with us as punkers for a Halloween party—a look Paul and I soon adopted as our regular appearance. We even got Mark to go dancing with us. Paul's brother John would buy us all the beer we wanted, and we'd drink as much as we could hold before going into the teen clubs, which only served sodas.

So much for the straight and narrow.

At one party, we decided it was time for Mark to learn to smoke pot. Paul showed him how to take a hit off his pipe, and as Mark was taking his first hit, my childhood friend John Barlow jumped on top of the fence above us and tried to scare us. When he realized what we were doing, John hightailed it out of there. It just so happened that as John sprang on us, I was taking the last swallow of my beer. I hurled my empty beer can at him and hit the target just as well as I had hit his sister Marianne's head with a snowball years earlier. The sound of the empty can bouncing off John's head sent Mark into a coughing fit, typical for someone getting high for the first time. Paul and I fell to the ground in hysterical laughter.

Mother Donna began to worry about Mark's association with Paul and me. Suddenly he wasn't allowed to go anywhere with us. It wasn't long after this that Mark came to me and said he loved me, but he couldn't hang out with us anymore because we were headed down a path he didn't want to take. He intended to stay on the straight and narrow. Mark and I slowly drifted apart as I sank deeper into the wild lifestyle I was chasing with every ounce of energy I could muster.

Paul and I had gotten so bold that we didn't care what Wayne or Mom thought and rebelled at every opportunity. Wayne blamed me for his son Paul's wild behavior, when the fact of the matter was that Paul was the one who introduced me to the vices I had become accustomed to. Wayne had no clue what was happening to his own son's life— something else that was familiar to me in a father-son relationship. One day, Wayne happened to be in town and graced Mom with his presence. He wasn't about to let the opportunity pass without trying to set his wayward stepson straight on a few things. When Wayne started in on me, it immediately erupted into a shouting match. I wasn't about take this from the man who habitually abandoned my mother and was in the dark about his own son.

As tempers flared I started to storm out of the room. Wayne shouted at me, "As long as I'm the man of this house, the conversation isn't over until I tell you it's over!"

I stopped in my tracks and turned around. Wayne began to smirk, thinking he had successfully exercised his authority over me. I paced over to him and stood with my face about five inches from his. "You aren't around here enough to lay claim to that title," I said in a calm matter-of-fact tone. "There's only one man in this room and it sure isn't you! If you doubt that fact, let's step outside."

Wayne's courage crumbled before me.

I crossed a line that day. I openly defied someone in authority over me for the first time in my life. And it felt good.

It wasn't long after my fight with Wayne that Mom decided she had endured enough of Wayne's indifference. She went to Alma Timpson of the Priesthood Council, and he gave her the release she needed from her marriage to Wayne on the grounds of neglect. Wayne never considered the release valid and to this day swears that my mother will be married to him in eternity because she didn't have biblical grounds for a release.

I bumped into Wayne shortly after Mom was granted her release. He started telling me how concerned he was about the path I was taking. Pointedly, he reminded me of Brigham Young's doctrine of blood atonement. Wayne told me how Porter Rockwell, an early follower of Joseph Smith and Brigham Young, used to take men who were worthy of being "blood atoned" out into the desert in the early days of Mormonism in Utah. Two men would head off together, but only Porter Rockwell would return. Wayne claimed that in some cases some men were so overtaken with guilt about their sins that they surrendered themselves voluntarily to have this ceremony performed. He described for me the detailed procedure for having their throats slit from ear to ear and their stomachs torn open so their entrails spilled out. I was completely disgusted and certain that he was just trying to frighten me. It never crossed my mind that the things he said were true. Nevertheless, a seed was planted in my mind that would bear fruit in my relationship with my own father.

But I wasn't going to listen to Wayne Horsley. He was nothing to me. I was my own man now.

I WAS in the middle of a raging teenage rebellion multiplied exponentially by my anger toward my father and growing resentment of the leaders of the FLDS. I was out of control, pure and simple.

And into the darkness, light shone.

I'll never forget the day years earlier that Howard came home specifically to announce he was a "born-again Christian." Father had always told us that born-again Christians think that just because they call upon Jesus to forgive them of their sins, they are forgiven and can go right back to their sinning and live however they want. They were free to be as wicked as they desired, and in the end, God would forgive them and let them into his heaven. But, of course, Father taught us that wasn't true. The truth was that born-again Christians would be limited in the afterlife to being single angels who are subject to the rule of those who progress to godhood. They exchanged a greater glory for a lesser glory and the things of this world.

Up to this point in my life I had never met a born-again Christian. What Howard was saying was like a bunch of scrambled connections in my brain. The family, though scattered from the farm, was in shock. How could Howard betray the family like this? Hadn't he listened when Father gave his long sermons about the "Great and Abominable Church," the "Whore of Babylon"? How could Howard join a Protestant church knowing what he knows about the truth? I could never bring myself to ask Howard what on earth he was thinking in becoming a Christian.

I remember when Howard came to me to talk about it personally; for the first time I can honestly say he was humble. It seemed odd to me that Howard was paying special attention to me at this moment; later I learned that he had gone to each of his siblings individually. He asked me about sin and what Jesus would have us do if we have sinned against someone. He talked to me about his realization that he was a sinner and in need of a Savior, and how he was able to receive forgiveness from God because of Jesus' death on the cross in atonement for those sins. God wanted Howard to seek out those whom he had sinned against and seek their forgiveness. My eyes glazed over; it was all so confusing! Then Howard got personal. He told me he knew how mean he had been to me in the past and asked if I could forgive him for the way that he had treated me.

I was shocked! It was all so overwhelming; I had no clue how to respond. What made Howard behave this way, and why did he need me to forgive him? I didn't want Howard to feel obligated to me somehow, so I forgave him, even though I really had no idea what he was talking about.

It never occurred to me that Howard had it right. I was having serious doubts about the FLDS and brazenly disobeyed rules at every opportunity. But still—become a *Christian?* I had never had a true burning in the bosom, so I understood why I might be a son of perdition, but Howard had said he did have a real testimony. So what happened? Did Howard comprehend that he would forever burn in the lake of fire? I shuddered at the thought that I might one day join him. I certainly seemed to be headed more in that direction than toward godhood.

There was one thing that I could say about Howard: As deceived as he might have been, he had something I didn't—*hope*, the kind that makes you sure something is true.

Howard was the first light of the gospel of Jesus Christ I ever saw being fleshed out in front of me. In Howard I saw the first evidence of a life being lived for Christ. Howard wasn't ashamed of his faith in Christ. He was bold in his witness. He wasn't arrogant in his attitude, but humbled himself so he could be a witness to the family. Howard didn't hide his faith from the world the way we hid ours in the FLDS; he displayed it for all to see. He didn't let people walk in and out of his life without sharing the love of Christ with them and making the appeal to them to start living for God. We were content to let outsiders go the way of the world; proselytizing was unheard of. We didn't send out missionaries to try and reach the lost; we were content that we were God's chosen people and didn't care what happened to the world outside. In fact, we were content to let go of many of our own young men.

The contrast was stark! Jesus said the good shepherd leaves the ninety-nine and goes out after the one that is lost. We didn't go out after the one that was lost unless it was a female. We drove men from our ranks to make room for worthy men to have multiple wives. How on earth was this supposed to be the loving God who sent his Son to die for our sins, only to have us driven out into the world to be eaten by wolves? Huge contradictions bombarded my brain that day and the weeks to follow, starting with the love Jesus so freely offers according to the Bible and the demands made to be worthy enough to receive that same love according to the FLDS faith. Howard's Jesus seemed easy to love, and to receive love from. Yet everything I'd ever been taught said that Howard was on the wide path that leads to destruction, and if I believed what he believed, I would be burning bridges that might one day take me back toward true salvation.

Despite Howard's effort, my rebellion raged on. By the time I was sixteen, my mother was thoroughly exasperated. She gave up trying to control me and sent me to live with Father in the hope that he would be able to keep me in line. I had not lived with Father for nearly three years, had next to no contact with him, and carried the anger of his absence from my childhood everywhere I went. In the intervening years, growing knowledge of the details of what he'd done to my sisters poured gasoline on the fire.

I took my punk leather and chains and moved back to Sandy. What good could possibly come from living with Father again?

13

Son of Perdition

But if ye neglect the tree, and take no thought for its
nourishment, behold it will not get any root; and when the
heat of the sun cometh and scorcheth it, because it hath no
root it withers away, and ye pluck it up and cast it out.

—*Book of Mormon, Alma 32:38*

My father didn't want me. He never had.

When my mother left him, she didn't ask Father for regular support. She left with nothing but her own ability to earn money. However, she did ask him to pay for some school clothes one time.

"You wanted him," he snapped. "You had him, you pay for him."

There it was: the admission that my father had never wanted me in the first place. My mother was the one who wanted to have another child, and I learned she tricked my father in order to get pregnant one last time.

That explained a lot. Fourteen years later, when we left, Father was still holding a grudge about my existence because he had never wanted me to come into the world in the first place.

But I *was* here. I *had* come into the world. Wasn't that worth anything? Father let Mom take me without a fight and didn't even want to pay for the clothes on my back. How could I feel anything but unloved, unwanted, and worthless? And now I had to go back and live in his house again.

When I first moved in with Father and Mother Midge, I was angry at my mom for sending me there. She knew I hated my father. She knew my soul boiled in fury over what he had done to my sisters. How could she send me to live there? Looking back, of course, I can see how desperate she must have been. At the time I was furious at what I thought was abandonment. I thought neither of my parents wanted me now.

But I didn't have a choice. And maybe it would be different. None of the other kids lived there anymore. It was just Father and Midge. None of my brothers had ever had the opportunity to live with Father without scads of other kids around. There would be no competition for his time and attention. Surely he would have time for me now.

As much as he didn't want me, Father really didn't have any choice about taking me in, any more than I had a choice about going. If Mom wanted to, she could take legal action against him for child support—he had never given her a dime—and it would all come out that he was a polygamist. So he agreed to have me to move back to the farm. I don't know why Mom thought things would be any different though; Father had never paid any attention to me, and from the outset he made it clear he had no plans to get involved with me now.

When I arrived, Father greeted me at the door. "Looks like you've got a bit of a five o'clock shadow there on your face. Are you shaving now?" he asked.

"Yeah," I said.

"How old are you now?" Father asked.

"Sixteen."

"Well, if you're old enough to shave, then you're old enough to do for yourself," he said. "I only have one rule; while you're living here, there is no smoking in my house."

"No problem," I said.

We both knew I was there because Mom couldn't handle me. Supposedly I needed someone to straighten me out. This was supposed to be the fatherly structure I needed? Complete independence with one meaningless rule? Why did I keep hoping he would care about me, with all the evidence stacking up that he didn't?

Father gave me the room in the farthest corner of the old boys' end of the basement, which was as far from him and Mother Midge as I could possibly get. There was some pretty clear symbolism in that choice. And because it was a basement room, I could come and go as I pleased through the bedroom window, just as I had as a child.

Nothing was really any different than it had been three years earlier when I left—except now I hated my father.

And I wanted him to love me.

And I hated that I wanted him to love me.

My anger multiplied by the day, but still I grasped at even the weakest straw, the remotest possibility that I might yet be able to have a relationship with my father. Occasionally I'd try to watch TV with him, but it was unimaginable to have a conversation that carried the inherent risk of talking about the family secret. Yet sitting there and not talking was intolerable. I spent most of my time in my room or out of the house completely.

Despite Father's one rule, cigarettes did me in. After a few months of living with Father—but rarely seeing him—I was arrested for stealing a carton of cigarettes, and Father had to come and rescue me from the police station.

"I guess I don't have to tell you how disappointed I am," he said.

"No, sir," I answered. I finally succeeded in getting his attention, and he was disappointed.

"At least you told the truth when you were caught," he said. "I know how addictive cigarettes are. If you can't afford them, just tell me. I'd rather buy them for you than have you steal them."

He made me promise that in exchange for speaking up for me in juvenile court, I would tell him when I needed cigarettes. However, the rule stood firm that I could not smoke in the house.

Ironically, after that, Father did try to reach out to me in his own way. Maybe he realized he was going to have to interact with me after all if I was going to get my life together. He took me bowling with him one Saturday. None of my brothers had ever gotten to go bowling with Father alone. This had the potential to be real one-on-one time, just Father and me. I hardly knew what to make of it! I had no other experiences to compare this with. But I went.

When we arrived at the bowling alley, Father asked me what type of beer I preferred to drink. Not exactly the action of a good Mormon father trying to spend time with his underage son. I specified Budweiser, and he went to the bar and came back with a pitcher of beer for us to share. I lit up a cigarette and Father did the same. It was strange to sit there and drink beer and smoke cigarettes with Father knowing the religious implications and how this violated the "Word of Wisdom" and therefore our worthiness. I was old enough now to see the outright hypocrisy of much of what Father did without any pretense of trying to make the pieces fit. What I had known intuitively growing up now was staring me in the face, and I was unabashedly participating.

IT WASN'T long before I broke that one rule, and Father made good on his word to kick me out. I'd lasted barely six months under Father's roof, I'm sure to my mother's dismay. In that time, we'd spent exactly two evenings together. I knew I would never live with Father again, never have the opportunity for a real relationship.

I bounced around after that, living a few months with my brother David, then with my sister Rena, then with Mom for a time, then on my own for a while.

Mom was terribly worried about me. Whenever I saw her, she would end up in tears about where my life was headed. I hated seeing her that way. Mark's comment about not wanting to go down the path I was on also rang in my mind. Despite the rebellion of my heart, my brain still believed the teaching I had received all my life: All other religions were lost, and the only hope for eternal salvation was through Mormonism. The fear for my soul was woven into my DNA and reared its ugly head again, and I decided to cover some bases by being rebaptized and reestablishing my status within the FLDS Church. Naturally this brought my mother great relief.

However, it didn't really change anything. I still couldn't get past the obvious misuse of authority for personal gain. By this time the Priesthood Council was an even two-against-two split, and I was beginning to get a glimpse of the power Rulon Jeffs craved. Uncle Roy's health continued to decline, leaving Rulon Jeffs to bombast the other Apostles and threaten the families of Colorado City with losing their homes if they followed Hammon and Timpson. I couldn't get past the lack of forgiveness shown to someone who was repentant. Even a genuinely repentant man had no chance of being restored to good standing. I couldn't get beyond how the past always haunted you; you could never be good enough to overcome the past and be free of it. I couldn't get any closer to God because of all the rules that had to be followed perfectly in order to be found worthy. And there remained my secret that I had never actually received a burning in the bosom. On the inside I was sure I was predestined to be a son of perdition, but I didn't dare speak those words aloud.

Out of frustration with all these things, I once again left the FLDS Church and began my quest to earn my spot in hell. I didn't want to go to hell just because God predestined it or because I couldn't gain the approval of the FLDS leaders. If I was going to hell, it would be my own choice to commit the sins that would get me there. I went wild all over again with Paul Horsley at my side. My sister Rena had left her husband, my stepbrother, and played country and western music in a band. I became a "roadie" for the band, which gave me access to the bars they frequented. Rena would sneak me beer or whiskey, and I would dance with all of her girlfriends. Before long, I was doing drugs stronger than pot—cocaine and crystal meth. With all its violently addictive qualities, crystal meth became my drug of choice.

I stopped paying bills and spent my money on food, gas, cigarettes, beer, and drugs. Mostly drugs, and more drugs. As a result, I got kicked out of my apartment and lost my car.

I was homeless. Actually homeless. What had I done with my life?

AFTER ONLY one terrifying night on the street, which convinced me I could never live that way, I called the one person I knew would take me in: my mother. She agreed to let me come and live with her, but I had to get myself together. So once again I straightened up and tried to fly right, rejoined the church, was rebaptized and began going to meetings again. Of course I had to choose which side of the ever-widening divide to be on. By this time, Uncle Roy had spoken publicly that he denounced

Alma Timpson and Marion Hammon, essentially exercising his power as president of the Priesthood Council to throw them off. They had moved a few miles from Colorado City to start their new group in Centennial Park. I chose to meet with Alma Timpson, who had looked kindly on my mother in her times of need. I explained the troubles I'd been through, the effect of my parents' divorce, Wayne's inability to accept me as a son, and my conflicted feelings toward my father. Brother Alma seemed to understand and empathize. He assured me God could forgive a repentant sinner. But I had to repent and never commit those sins again, or all my past sins would once again be on my shoulders.

I was old enough now to start thinking about marriage. If I was going to rejoin the fundamentalist polygamists, then I would need to continue my path to godhood by plural marriage. So I asked Alma Timpson what I would have to do to be allowed to take a wife. He calmly explained that there weren't enough women to go around, and if I wanted to marry, I would have to go out into the world to convert a woman to polygamy and bring her back.

I was shocked. I wasn't given a list of things to do in order to be worthy. At that moment in time, I would have agreed to anything. Instead, I was saddled with the one thing that was virtually impossible to do. The message was clear: I wasn't worthy of a wife from the polygamous community. I had been blackballed. I knew Uncle Roy and Rulon Jeffs would not have a more favorable opinion. The leaders would never approve me for marriage, so no father would want to give his daughter to me. I had already proven I was a flight risk by leaving twice before. They had only gone through the motions of taking me back and rebaptizing me. The truth was I would never be allowed to participate fully in the community through plural marriage.

I knew that some boys younger than I was literally had been dropped off in the streets of St. George, Utah, and told never to come back. They hadn't done that to me, but the end result was the same. I was not a "favored son" and would not be receiving a daughter of Zion to take for a wife. Thus my progress toward a celestial kingdom was at a dead stop.

The universal, deep-seated teaching for boys in the FLDS Church is that they would grow up and become polygamists themselves. This is the path to godhood; there is no other way. This was the bedrock of everything we were taught about religion. Little boys, though, don't understand the mathematics of it. They don't understand that for the system to work, many of them will have to leave so the men who remain can have plural wives. In their teen years, boys begin to come up against the truth that polygamy will damn more men than it will save. Those who fail to be found worthy will be damned in their progression to godhood, and there really is no point in staying in the community.

So there I was, nineteen years old and faced with the truth that I had no hope of ever being worthy of a daughter of Zion.

Nineteen years old with no hope of redemption from the weight of my past.

Nineteen years old and a history of sins that could not be overcome.

Nineteen years old and a boiling hatred for my own father because he had never been a father to me and had been a predator to my sisters.

WHEN MY sisters finally opened up and let Father's dark secret out, Father maintained his innocence concerning the charges. Rena later shared with me her experience from her sixteenth birthday celebration. It had become tradition that Father would take his daughters on a dinner date on their sixteenth birthday. On the drive home Father told Rena about an educational course he would be teaching to prepare his daughters for marriage.

This course was private, with Father as the instructor, and completion of the course would propel Rena in her status to being equal with Father's wives. In fact, she would be like a sister-wife to them. The language was clear: This would be a sex education course with hands-on, practical application. Rena tried very hard at first to tell her experiences of sexual abuse in ways that were polite and without graphic detail. Unfortunately, the evidence wasn't specific enough, wasn't graphic enough, wasn't convincing enough for many in the family. As a result, the family had a hard time coming to grips with the accusations leveled against Father, even though Mary, Kathleen, and Laura confirmed everything Rena said and added stories of their own. Many called them liars without even hearing their side of the story. They completely dismissed their charges as false allegations without ever hearing the real evidence that only a graphic telling would provide.

My sisters were going through therapy to help them deal with the impact of Father's abuse, and added to the already heavy weight upon their shoulders was having their family abandon them and brand them as liars. Because they were seeking therapy, some of the family claimed that they were mentally unstable and therefore lying about Father as an attempt to get attention. Of course, for me the question always arose, Who in the world would seek that kind of attention? I for one could not help but believe them. I was there and heard their horrific stories and comforted them when they broke down crying because of what they had experienced. Many of their stories were too real, too filled with details and real emotions to possibly be a lie.

Psychologists have noted that of all the memory stimulators, the sense of smell is the strongest. One of my sisters once told me that when her son became an unruly teenager and started smoking, she had to ask him to change his cologne. He wore Brut, and the combination of cigarette smoke and Brut cologne reminded her of Father. Father wore Brut cologne and smoked too. He had forced her to give him oral sex, and today whenever she smells the combination of Brut cologne and cigarette smoke, it takes her back to the ugly past. The image was forever burned in my mind of just what kind of monster Father had become.

I hated my father.

I hated him for not being there for me.

I hated him for never wanting me.

I hated him for what he had done to my sisters and what a hypocrite he was about it.

I hated being obligated emotionally to be there for my sisters who would cry their eyes out on my shoulder about the horrors they endured.

I hated the injustice. I wanted their pain to end.

Of all the people that I had ever known, Father seemed a worthy candidate for that "blood atonement" Wayne had talked about a few years earlier. The hate inside me pulsated, pounded, throbbed its way out of my soul. I didn't know how long I would be able to contain it. For my own sake I needed to get away from everything and everyone I knew.

So I joined the U.S. Navy.

And that's how I ended up in a naval hospital talking to a psychiatrist about wanting to kill my father.

14

Join the Navy, See the World

*All mankind love themselves, and ... he would be glad to
have his blood shed. That would be loving themselves, even
unto an eternal exaltation. Will you love your brothers
and sisters likewise, when they have committed a sin
that cannot be atoned for without the shedding of their
blood? Will you love that man or woman well enough
to shed their blood? That is what Jesus Christ meant.*

—Brigham Young, Journal of Discourses,
vol. 4, pp. 219–20

For a young man who grew up as insulated as I did, the navy was
about as far away from the FLDS as I could imagine. Even my
teen punk rebellion years paled in comparison. In those years I hadn't
wandered far from home geographically, and though I flagrantly
abused every boundary around me, the FLDS still encompassed the
anchors of my life. My family was around, the Apostles were there, I
could go back if I wanted to. In the navy, the safety net was gone.

Even if I'd stayed home and remained in the FLDS, life would have been in upheaval. Uncle Roy died in 1986, the same year I joined the navy at nineteen. The rift that had been straining the fabric of the Priesthood Council for years finally rent it in two. Having usurped the status of president and Prophet for himself, Rulon Jeffs began to clean the dissenters out of the community by taking their homes from them and assigning them to saints who sided with him. My years in the navy were the same years that Rulon Jeffs, with his son Warren in the wings, consolidated his power and became even more heavy-handed than the leaders before him. Eventually he moved his own family from the Salt Lake Valley to Colorado City where he could better control the core community there. He shut down his large complex in the mouth of Little Cottonwood Canyon where we had gathered for Sunday meetings. Reconciliation with Rulon Jeffs being impossible, Apostles Marion Hammon and Alma Timpson pursued their own community in nearby Centennial Park.

In the navy I became an aviation structural mechanic working specifically on ejection seats. When my training was complete, I was assigned to a base in California, and I was eager to go.

California was great! I jumped right into the party scene with both feet. After all, I was headed for hell anyway; I was a "son of perdition," an apostate, someone who had the light of the Mormon gospel revealed to him and had turned from it. If I was going to burn in hell, I at least wanted some good memories. I got a motorcycle and drove it furiously on the San Diego highways. I wasn't concerned about the future, where I was going, or how I was going to get there. If it had alcohol in it, I drank it. If it was an illegal drug, I used it. If it wore a skirt, I slept with it. My crystal-meth addiction continued to wreak havoc in my life. Many of my friends warned me that if I didn't stop, the Naval Command would catch me on a urinalysis.

I didn't stop.

Officers knew I was using but couldn't prove it, and it was just a matter of time before they caught me. I knew that.

But I didn't stop.

Informants would warn me whenever they knew a urinalysis was coming up, and I had learned how to clean out my system rapidly so that I could pass the test. I was living as hard and fast as I could.

I didn't stop. I didn't want to stop. If I stopped, I might feel something I didn't want to feel.

While stationed in San Diego, I discovered I had a cousin named Natalie, my mother's sister Arlene's daughter, who lived with her husband in the area. We had not grown up together, so we had a lot of catching up to do. I would go over to their place from time to time and visit. I called them one day to find out what their plans were for the weekend. Natalie informed me that Aunt Donna was in town visiting them. I asked if I could come over because it had been years since I had seen Mother Donna, and Natalie agreed. So I jumped on my motorcycle and headed out to their house. When I arrived, I visited with Natalie while I waited for Mother Donna to come out of her room.

"So, Brian," Natalie asked me, "what do you think about your new stepfather?"

"What!" I exclaimed.

The shock on Natalie's face could not have been more telling than my own.

"You hadn't heard?" she said.

"Heard what? Who got married?" My pulse quickened. Natalie must have just found out Mother Donna had gotten married.

"Your mother didn't tell you?"

"Tell me what?"

"Oh boy," Natalie said, embarrassed. "I guess I just let the cat out of the bag."

"Natalie, stop talking in riddles. Who is this new stepfather, and which one of my mothers did he marry?" I insisted. "Was it Mother Donna?"

"No, it wasn't Aunt Donna," she said.

My heart sank in my chest. The process of elimination didn't take long. Mother Midge was still married to Father, and Mother Maurine had died of lung cancer a few years earlier. The only possible candidate was my mother.

"Are you saying my mother got married?" I asked.

"I'd better let Aunt Donna tell you. I don't think it would be right for you to hear it from me."

I paced the floor waiting for Mother Donna to make her entrance. When she saw me, her face lit up and we hugged each other. As soon as the pleasantries were over, though, I set out to get some answers.

"What's this I hear about my mother getting married?" I asked.

"Oh my," Mother Donna said, "you mean your mother didn't tell you?"

"Obviously it slipped her mind!" I exclaimed. "How long has she been married?"

"She's been married to Sterling for about a month now," she informed me.

"Wait a minute! I talked to her less than two weeks ago and she didn't bother to tell me that she had gotten married? She couldn't have told me herself?"

"Brian, Sterling seems to be a very good man," Mother Donna said, trying to reassure me.

"Sterling who?" I asked. "Does he have a last name?"

"Tolman."

"Is he a polygamist?"

"Sterling came out of the LDS Church and has become a convert," she said. "He already had a wife, and now that he has married your mother, he is a polygamist."

As if that softened the blow! I didn't like the idea of my mother marrying another polygamist. I had hoped that she would have seen these people for what they are—frauds, people who use religion to manipulate other people. If he was a polygamist then he was no good. I was a grown man, but another polygamist husband would try to assert his authority over me. The last thing in the world I wanted was another father figure trying to boss me around or telling me how to live. I had already made my mind up that I didn't like this Sterling Tolman.

"Perhaps you should call your mother and let her fill you in on all the details," Mother Donna suggested.

All I could think about for the rest of the day was how my mother could get married and not bother to tell me. At least she could have told me on the phone when I talked to her earlier, but no! Instead she intentionally kept it a secret from me. If I hadn't happened to call Natalie, and if Mother Donna hadn't happened to be visiting, I still would not know. I was shocked, hurt, and offended in the extreme.

As soon as I returned to the barracks, I phoned Mom. She explained how they met, his conversion to the fundamental teachings of Mormonism, and how his wife also accepted them. Nothing she said could persuade me to accept Sterling. I wasn't going to open myself up to another stepfather who was just going to turn out to be a jerk like Wayne.

I was free from all the garbage I was raised with. I was in the navy now; I was far away from the family, and that was the way I liked it. But somehow learning that my mother had once again embroiled herself in plural marriage stirred my latent anger about the polygamous community in general and my father in particular.

My entire time in the navy became a blur of alcohol and crystal meth. Time flew by, and before I knew it, I was only six months from the end of my enlistment.

WHILE I wanted nothing to do with the family structures and the FLDS Church, I did care about my sisters. Throughout the years I had always tried to make myself available to them if they needed a shoulder to cry on or wanted to talk about things they needed to get off their chests. The more I heard of their stories, the angrier I became with my father. Hate ballooned into intention to do something about it, to make him pay, to get even for the pain he had caused.

I wanted to kill my father.

What my sisters needed was justice to help them heal the wounds of the past; certainly killing Father would make their pain go away.

I purchased a handgun, which I stored in the base armory. I could check my gun out of the armory and take it into the desert, where I pinned pictures of Father to a cardboard box and practiced shooting. At first it was just a way to vent my anger. But the more I vented, the more attractive the real act became. I began thinking about how I would do it—what method I could use that would have the greatest impact. The closer I came to being discharged from the navy, the more my plan came into focus.

I happened to be exiting the navy on Father's Day. Father had traded the big house and farm in Sandy to another polygamist for a home in the polygamist community of Colorado City, Arizona, which was owned by the United Effort Plan. This was only about a seven-hour drive from San Diego. I figured I could drive to Colorado City the same day I got out of the navy, arrive late at night, sneak into the house, and kill Father in his sleep. Killing him on Father's Day would be suitably ironic.

But just in case there was an iota of truth in the doctrine of blood atonement, I talked myself into believing I was doing this for his own good. The sins he had committed were beyond the redeeming work of Christ. He had to pay for them with his own blood. Even though my father had never wanted me, even though he had marginalized me my whole life, I had the power to redeem him. I could fulfill the Mormon theology drilled into me and love my father in the ultimate way, and at the same time Father would get what he deserved.

Just killing him wasn't enough, though. I wanted the world to know why.

Upon moving to Colorado City, Father had become the facilities manager for the Leroy S. Johnson Meeting House, the community center where they held their Sunday morning worship services. This was the perfect venue for publicly announcing the sins that merited blood atonement. I could spray-paint a message on the side of the community center in Colorado City the night I killed my father. I would write "Clyde Mackert is a child molester" on the side of the building where everyone would see it and know the truth.

I didn't care what happened to me. It didn't matter if I lived or died or went to jail—I was a son of perdition anyway.

While I was in the throes of torment about blood atoning my father and getting justice at the same time, I received the news that Grandma Rhea had passed away. I put in for emergency leave and traveled home for her funeral. While I was there, I spent a lot of time with my sisters, and their pain only reinforced my resolve. Father still denied everything.

Our half siblings believed my sisters were sick liar apostates. Several of my sisters had even contacted law officials over the years and gotten no response. The extensive therapy they were undergoing was bringing to the surface horrifying specific memories. Every time I talked to one of them, the picture became uglier and the need for justice magnified.

Even during leave for my grandmother's funeral, I continued to use drugs and alcohol to self-medicate and cope with my tangle of emotions. But the emotions were surging more powerfully every day. Seven generations of breeding and modeling to subdue and control emotions was no longer enough to make me ignore what I felt: pure, undiluted rage.

I had a gym bag packed with everything I would need to carry out my plan. It was time to do it. Fantasy was rapidly becoming reality.

When I returned from my emergency leave, I discovered my unit was having a urinalysis—and my number had come up. I had a bad feeling my bottle would be among those actually tested this time. I put off the urinalysis as long as I could. Finally I was ordered not to leave the hanger until I supplied the sample. Obviously they knew I was on drugs and were determined to corner me on it. The moment came when admitting I had a problem and getting help didn't seem so outlandish. After all, running from my problems had only gotten me closer to killing my father.

I summoned the courage for what I needed to do and went to my supervisor to inform him I needed help. I had been doing drugs to cope with the issues of abuse in my family, and I was planning to kill my father. He escorted me up to the chaplain's office to let me get things off my chest while he continued to the Command Senior Chief to inform him of my situation. They sent me home to the barracks, placed me under suicide watch, and arranged an appointment with a doctor at

Balboa Naval Hospital's mental health ward. And that was what had brought me to this series of appointments with the psychiatrist.

I entered the doctor's office, sat in the usual chair, had the usual glass of water, exchanged the usual greetings, answered the usual questions about my state of mind, and waited for him to start asking new questions.

"Well, Brian, I think we've made significant progress so far," he said. "I want you to know your thoughts and feelings toward your father are normal and natural. Anyone who has been through what you have gone through would be wrestling with the same things you've been wrestling with. I just have a few questions for you. Let's suppose hypothetically for a moment that you acted on your homicidal thoughts toward your father, that you didn't just plan his murder, but that you followed through with it and executed the plan. What do you think that it would accomplish?"

"Justice! It would give my sisters the justice they aren't going to get from the law," I asserted.

"Yes, it would," he acknowledged, "but what would be the consequence besides achieving justice on their behalf? What would happen to you afterward?"

"I would certainly go to prison," I admitted.

"Yes, that is a very likely possibility," he agreed. "Are you prepared to go to prison? Is it really worth it?"

"I'm not fond of being someone's wife in prison, if that's what you mean," I said. "I would rather die."

"Well, then, is it worth throwing away your life for?" he asked.

"I don't know." My resolve was beginning to waver.

"Let's look at it from the perspective of what you could possibly gain rather than what you stand to lose," he suggested. "Would killing your father reduce the pain that your sisters are experiencing?"

I thought about that for a while. "No," I answered, "I suppose it wouldn't because the damage has already been done."

"If it wouldn't reduce their pain, would it increase their pain?" he asked. "How do you think it would make your sisters feel if you killed your father and either ended up in prison as a result or you killed yourself rather than be arrested? Would that decrease or increase their pain?"

I hadn't really thought about that aspect of it. My fantasy had only taken me to the moment of justice for my sisters. "I imagine it would increase their pain," I conceded.

"Why?"

"Because on top of the pain of what my father has done to them, their baby brother is now in prison or dead as a result of trying to ensure they got justice. The situation would only become more complicated for them emotionally."

"Do you think that they might experience some level of self-imposed guilt because it was what happened to them that drove you to kill your father?"

"I suppose there would be some level of regret or self-inflicted guilt as a result."

"So rather than solving the problem by killing your father, you would actually be making the problem worse for them. Is that what you're saying?"

"Yeah, that's right," I admitted.

"Let me ask you another question, then," he said. "Are you in any way to blame for what your father did to them?" he asked.

"No! Father is!"

"If you aren't a part of the problem, and if you aren't to blame for your father's behavior, then are you a part of the solution to the problem?"

"No, I suppose not."

"Brian, your sisters have been hurt by your father's behavior at a level you don't have the ability to make right," the doctor said. "And it isn't your responsibility to make it right. Be there for them when they need you, but also know when you can't take it and need a break yourself."

He paused to let his words sink in. He was right. I had been so enraged on behalf of my sisters that I had lost perspective on what my hate was doing to me.

"Let me pose another question," he said. "Do you worry that because your father was a child molester you will end up being one as well?"

"Well, yeah, I suppose in a way I do," I confessed. My deepest darkest fear was that somehow because of who my father was, I was destined to become the same monster. I had already decided I didn't want children. I would never get married and have a family, because the one sure way not to turn into my father was not to have a child.

"Brian, just because your father was a child molester doesn't mean you will be one as well," he said. "Who your father was doesn't define who you are going to be. You have the ability to choose for yourself what you will or won't be in the future. You can walk out these doors today and continue to let the events of the past dictate your future for you. Or you can go out those doors and create a whole new future for yourself. It's really up to you. What type of future do you want for yourself, Brian? I'm giving you permission to make the future whatever you want it to be."

I looked at the door, an ordinary office door. On the other side lay my future. I wanted to believe what the doctor was saying, that I could create a whole new future for myself. I didn't have to take ownership of what my father had done. That wasn't what defined me or made me who I am; I could choose a better future.

That's exactly what I decided to do.

The doctor's cognitive approach made sense to me. Killing my father wouldn't solve anything; in fact, it would make things worse. My FLDS breeding had taught me to subdue my emotions. For a while, I almost lost my logical grip, but now I had it back. Coming to a pragmatic decision about why I should not kill my father gave me the strength to once again subdue my homicidal intentions.

There was just one problem: I still hated my father. Father's life was safe, but mine was the same mess it had always been.

15

The Few, the Proud—the Father

How beautiful are the feet of those who bring good news!

—Romans 10:15

I didn't go to Colorado City when I left the navy on June 16, 1990. It was a long time before I saw my father again. It was just better that way.

I moved in with my sister Rena to try to get my feet on the ground and make a life for myself. Unfortunately, I discovered that what I had trained for in the navy did not translate all that well to the civilian aviation industry. I ended up working in construction, the only other job skill I had. However, the housing industry was not exactly robust at the time, either. I went through the cycle of getting hired and laid off eleven times in nine months. My eyes turned back to the military. This time, though, I wanted to be sure I came out of it with job expertise for which there was demand in the private sector. Rather than just enlisting in the navy to escape a life I had come to hate, as I did when I was nineteen, I did my research. Both the army and the marines looked appealing, but

I finally decided I wanted to join the marines and work in communications to learn skills I was sure the real world needed.

But first, because I didn't have a high school diploma, I needed a General Equivalency Diploma. So, off I went to Brigham Young University in Provo, Utah, to take the GED test. Without any preparation or studying, I walked in, sat down, and took the test. I figured that if I failed, at least I would know what areas I needed to work on. To my amazement, I passed! In fact, my score was right up there with the top 12 percent of high school graduates who took the exam to verify its reliability. I guess Mother Donna was right when she said that the quality of education we got at Mountain View Academy was equal to or greater than most high schools!

Joining the marines also meant repeating boot camp, since theirs was longer than the navy's, and the marines was the only branch of the military that didn't accept completion of another branch's boot camp.

The night before I left for boot camp, I sat with my sister Mary in her car saying good-bye. Mary had left her polygamous husband, Bill Draper, some time earlier. At first, she had gone wild with her new-found freedom. But she had her five boys to look after, and that kept her in line. One of her sons played on a sports team, and the coach was a Christian. Apparently he and Mary engaged in some heated discussions. Mary defended Mormonism, and the coach explained why Mormonism wasn't and couldn't be restored Christianity. He challenged her one day to go downtown to the Salt Lake Temple and study the arches over the doors. Mary did—and she found pentagrams and other occult symbols. The coach asked her how a Christian church could have occult symbols on what it considers to be the holiest of places. Not long after, Mary renounced Mormonism. She tired of trying to be good enough to earn her salvation. Instead, she gave her heart to the Savior who could forgive all of her sins and began attending a Christian church for the first time.

Sitting in Mary's car that night, I melted down. Racked with pain over a father who didn't love me, a family that was distant and divided, and the anger I still harbored for my father's crimes against his daughters—I was a wreck! I was about to go off and become a member of "the few, the proud, the marines," and I was sobbing in my sister's car over the compounded grief that constituted my life.

As I spilled my guts and sobbed, Mary listened—and assured me she knew everything I was feeling. She had lived through it all herself, and the Mormons had it wrong. The only way she ever found to heal those wounds was through Jesus Christ. God had become the Father she never had; Jesus had healed her wounds. I could have the same thing, she urged me, if I surrendered my life to him and accepted the free gift of eternal life. I could do it right then, sitting with her in the car.

I would have none of it.

Because of the whole priesthood-headship trip that the FLDS had bred into me, I hated the thought of organized religion and being under someone else's authority. I thought if I asked Jesus to come into my life and heal my wounds the way Mary wanted me to, I would be placed under her authority, or her pastor's authority. I had seen religion used to manipulate and control, to gain power, even to line the pockets of a few. I didn't want any of it!

"I don't know if there even is a God," I ranted to Mary, "and if there is, I hate him for letting these things happen in our family. I'll curse him to his face if he's real."

Mary responded with a statement I didn't understand at the time. She said that one day I would come to know God the way she knew him, and when I did, he would become the Father I never had—a faithful

Father, a loving Father, a kind Father, a forgiving Father. A Father to the fatherless.

I said my final good-bye to my sister and got out of the car thinking that if there was a God, he had forsaken me, so why should I call on him?

Despite my determination to turn my back on God, however, while I was in boot camp, I couldn't resist the growing sense that I needed God in my life somehow. Mary's words rang in my heart—that God could be the Father to the fatherless.

That was me. Fatherless.

When missionaries from the LDS Church crossed my path, I willingly talked with them. At least it was familiar to me. I knew for certain I was not going back to the FLDS, and the kind of churches that my siblings Howard and Mary went to—well, I wouldn't know what to do in a place like that. Even as my hatred simmered, logic swelled, and I reasoned that perhaps after all this time, it was the FLDS that got things wrong, and the LDS Church had things right all along. Maybe the FLDS were the ones who were defying God. At least I recognized the crux of the LDS Church and knew how to hook myself to something there. To my shock as much as anyone's, I decided to join the mainstream LDS Church.

After boot camp, the marines sent me to Twentynine Palms, California, to the Marine Corps Air Ground Command Center for training in radio communications. The next step was orders for Okinawa, Japan. I was going to see a part of the world no one in my family had ever been to. I had to learn all of the aircraft identification and rules of engagement, how to track targets, and fire missiles. Still looking for God to prove himself to me and mean something, I went to a few of the LDS Church services in Okinawa. With my seven-generation Mormon pedigree, I knew more about LDS Church history than most Mormons, and I was really annoyed with the way the LDS Church rewrote history to make it more palatable to the masses. Mormon history was my family history. When they rewrote Mormon history, they rewrote my family history, and I couldn't swallow it. They had nothing for me there, so I stopped going.

So much for looking for God.

In Okinawa you can spend your time three ways: Drink yourself silly, get religion, or become a physical-fitness freak. I'd had enough of being a drunk during my navy years, and I also had my fill of religion, so I began to spend all my time in the gym. When I'd shipped out to Okinawa, I'd left behind a fiancée, and despite my skirt-chasing history, I was determined to be faithful. I was going to get a grip on my life somehow. So I stuck to the gym and made it through my one-year tour of duty.

Before I knew it, the year was over and my orders for my next duty station had come in. I was headed to Marine Corps Air Station in Cherry Point, North Carolina. Back stateside, I discovered that my fiancée had not had the same resolve I'd had. Her unfaithfulness meant the end of our relationship, and I didn't date anyone else for a year and a half. I was not anxious to complicate my life again with another relationship. In the FLDS we didn't date, so when I hit the outside world, I thought the whole purpose of dating was the sexual conquest, and I became pretty good at that end of things. My dating history had consisted of picking up women in bars and having sexual relationships with them that occasionally turned into emotional relationships. But these relationships didn't work because they had been based on sex in the first place, not friendship or feelings of love. The thrill had worn off. For a long time, I just didn't want to do it. Instead, I kept my nose to the grindstone in the marines and made corporal, and then sergeant.

Shortly after becoming a sergeant, though, my dating dry spell was coming to an end. Ready for a social life once again, I started going to Greenville, North Carolina, to go dancing. Eastern Carolina University was in Greenville, and a college town was a productive place to meet women. Greenville had a great bar called the Texas Two Step, which housed two different themes in one place. One half was a country and western bar, the other half was a rock 'n' roll bar; a pool hall divided the two. I met a lot of people there and soon had several regular dance partners.

While hanging out at the Texas Two Step, I noticed an attractive woman who almost always came in by herself. One night I arrived in Greenville early and was killing time waiting for the crowd to show up and the action to begin, so I had a few beers and shot some pool. Just before things got going in the club, this woman came in and went up to the bar to order a beer. I watched her walk past me, and when I finished my beer, I turned around to buy another beer at the same time she was turning to leave the bar. We both stopped just short of crashing into each other.

"Hello," she said looking up at me and smiling.

My heart skipped a beat. I could have sworn I meant to say hello, but "Ugh" was all that came out of my mouth. I watched her walk away and go to the rock 'n' roll side of the bar. She looked up at me a few times and noticed I was watching her. On the side of the stage, she was dancing by herself in front of the mirrors. Just then Tim McGraw's "Don't Take the Girl" came on. I knew a unique dance called "The Sway" for this song. I finally found my tongue as I approached the mesmerizing young woman.

"Would you like to dance?" I asked.

"Sure," she said.

"Do you know how to do 'The Sway'?"

"No."

"Would you like to learn it?"

"Sure."

"The Sway" is a couple's dance where the man dances behind the woman but very close to her. If done correctly with lots of eye contact, it is very romantic. We danced staring into each other's eyes. When the song was over, we struck up a conversation. Her name was Dana, and she was a student at the university. Dana and I hit it off and spent every moment together from that night on. Our relationship followed my usual pattern of the past, but the more I was with her, the more I knew this one would be different. I'd spent enough time alone in the last year and a half, getting to know myself and figuring out what I wanted in a wife, to see that Dana had the whole package. And the tender way she cared for the menagerie of animals in her life persuaded me she'd be a great mother, too.

I was completely smitten, and three weeks after we met, I popped the question. Fast? Yes. But by FLDS standards, an eternity. Most of my siblings and the people I grew up with got only a few days notice that they were getting married, and they were often married to people they didn't know as well as I knew Dana. I was making headway in the marines, and I didn't spend every waking moment drunk the way I had in the navy. I was making something of my life. I was twenty-seven years old and thought I knew what I wanted—and Dana was it. It made perfect sense to me to get married and settle down. Eighty-two days after we met, we were married.

While we were moving into the new apartment that base housing arranged for us, Dana became sick and was throwing up constantly. Two weeks after we were married we found out she was pregnant.

I was going to be a father!

What did I know about being a father? I was still wishing I had a real father myself, and now I was going to be one. The navy psychiatrist had helped me see I didn't have to let my own childhood define me, that I could make different choices when it came to being a husband and father. Now suddenly the test was staring me in the face.

Obviously my own father was no help in showing me how to be a father—except to do the opposite of everything he did. My first stepfather, Wayne Horsley, had been a big disappointment. My second stepfather, Sterling Tolman had given me some hope it was possible to be a good father. Though he was a polygamist, and as hard as I'd resisted liking him, Sterling had a lot of appealing qualities. He was kind and gentle but could be firm when the situation called for it. Sterling worked with troubled kids in Job Corps and was equipped for helping kids—like Mackert kids—deal with emotional issues. And he had been a wonderful husband to my mother.

I came to know and respect Sterling as an adult. But what in the world was I going to do with a baby?

DANA AND I began looking at all of the things that would change in our lives when we became parents. Neither of us had been living a life pleasing to God. We'd never even really talked about religion before this, but we both felt a responsibility to teach our child something about God. But what? I was raised a Mormon and she was raised a Baptist.

"So what do Mormons believe?" Dana asked.

I didn't take the route that the missionaries often took in explaining how Joseph Smith claimed to have restored the true Christian Church via revelations and visitations from God, Jesus, and angels. Instead, I simply stuck to what all Mormons believe and are striving for: godhood. This is what my whole life in the FLDS had been about. I explained this core teaching starting with the war in heaven that resulted in one-third of the hosts of heaven being worthy to receive white and delightsome physical bodies in which to progress toward godhood.

After I finished, Dana said, "Wow! I think I understand, but I need some time to process it all. I'm going to sleep on it and we'll talk again in the morning."

In the morning Dana informed me she would never become a Mormon. When I asked her why, she told me, "According to the Bible there has only ever been one God, there weren't any gods formed before him, and there will not be any gods formed after him."

"Where do you find that in the Bible?" I asked. Mormons used the Bible, but I had never heard this teaching.

"Right here in Isaiah 43:10," she said, opening her Bible to Isaiah. "'You are my witnesses,' declares the Lord, 'and my servant whom I have chosen, so that you may know and believe me and understand that I am he. Before me no god was formed, nor will there be one after me.'"

I read the verse and stood there baffled. This one verse held the power to destroy everything that I had ever been taught growing up as a Mormon. All my concepts of who God was and who I was before him were destroyed, gone in the instant my gentle wife read me that verse.

The whole notion that God was once a man who worked his way to godhood—gone!

The idea that I could someday become a god myself through righteous living according to the laws and ordinances of the gospel—gone!

Everything I thought I knew about the godhead—gone!

Never before had a verse from the Bible impacted me this

profoundly. In the Mormon godhead the Father, Son, and Holy Spirit are three separate beings who are one in mind and purpose only, yet all three are separate beings, and separate gods. How could they possibly be separate gods if there were no gods formed before or after God the Father? The only way that Jesus and the Holy Ghost could be separate beings or separate gods is if all three of them, the Father, the Son, and the Holy Ghost, all became gods at the exact same moment in time! Yet that wasn't possible because Jesus was the spirit-child of God the Father after he had already attained godhood. In Mormon teaching, it isn't known when the Holy Ghost became a god, but I could definitely put my finger on Jesus and say that his godhood came after God the Father's, because Jesus was God's first spirit-child.

Dana went on and showed me another verse from Isaiah that further dizzied my world: "Do not tremble, do not be afraid. Did I not proclaim this and foretell it long ago? You are my witnesses. Is there any God besides me? No, there is no other Rock; I know not one" (Isa. 44:8).

In this verse God says that he knows of no other gods. If God the Father, who is all-knowing, knows of no other gods, how could he possibly have a Father God? If he did, then he was denying his Father-God, which is a damnable sin according to God's own law. How could God remain holy and righteous while denying the existence of his Father-God, thereby violating his own law; yet at the same time condemning us to an eternal hell if we deny our own Father-God?

Everything I ever knew to be true—whether or not I lived up to it—crumbled as these two verses slammed together in my head.

After regaining my composure, I said, "As long as we go to a church that teaches from the Bible that Jesus is the Son of God who came and died for my sins and was raised from the grave, I don't have a problem with it." Of course, what those phrases actually meant to me at the time was up for discussion.

Dana and I agreed that we would concentrate on the things we needed to do to prepare for the birth of our child and put off looking for a church until after the baby was born. I was ecstatic and petrified at the same time. The psychiatrist in San Diego had helped me see I wasn't doomed to become a pedophile, but I certainly wasn't equipped to be a father, either. Growing up, the model of marriage before me was that as long as husbands didn't beat their wives or cheat on them, as long as they provided and kept a roof over the family, then the wives had nothing to complain about. Anything the women might have been feeling was irrelevant. The men knew it, the women knew it, and the children learned it. I never saw a moment of affection between my father and any of his wives. Fathers were authority figures who struck fear in their children's hearts. Fathers were people who disappeared for long hours and left the work of raising children to the women.

I had just gotten married and was still figuring out what being a husband outside the FLDS meant, and now I was going to be a father, too.

The Marine Corps in all its wisdom decided to send me back to Okinawa for a year—without Dana and before the baby was born. I wasn't about to miss the birth of my child and the first year of his life. My child would not grow up thinking his father was distant and wanted nothing to do with him. To avoid this separation, I pressed for a different assignment. I could take my family with me to Okinawa if I reenlisted and agreed to serve a three-year tour in Japan, beginning after the baby was born. We took the deal. Dana hadn't been to Japan before, but she was eager to experience the Japanese culture firsthand.

The baby went past his due date, and Dana didn't go into labor until April 1, about two weeks late. Twelve hours later, the doctor announced that it was her medical opinion that taking the baby by cesarean section would be best, and Dana agreed. She wanted this over! They positioned me at Dana's head; neither Dana nor I could see the actual procedure, but only moments later, the doctor announced, "It's a boy!"

I started to stand and look, but Dana grabbed my arm, "No, don't look at him until we can see him together. I want to see your face when you look at him for the first time." I sat back down, wanting to honor her tender request.

"Brian, would you like to cut the umbilical cord?" the doctor asked.

I looked at Dana. "I only get one chance to do this," I said.

"Go ahead," she said.

A nurse was busy cleaning up my son. He was crying loudly with his eyes closed and his fists clenched. He was the prettiest sight I had ever seen. I took his hands and counted his fingers, then moved to his toes; he was perfect! The nurse directed me to where I needed to make the cut, and with the scissors she provided, I cut the cord. I stood there in awe of my son and held his little hand. He clutched it tightly and my heart was no longer my own; from that moment on it was his.

"What's his name?" the nurse asked me with her pen poised over an identification card.

"He is Sterling Edward Mackert," I said. I leaned over and whispered in his ear, "That's right; you are Sterling Edward Mackert, the keeper of my heart, and my little April fool." Dana had always wanted to name a child Sterling, and I was happy to honor my stepfather who had turned out to be a wonderful man.

In that instant, an emotionally fatherless polyg kid gave his heart away to his own offspring. An angry marine glimpsed the real meaning of life. Nothing would ever be the same.

But the real change was yet to come.

16

Road to Damascus

For if you forgive men when they sin against
you, your heavenly Father will also forgive
you. But if you do not forgive men their sins,
your Father will not forgive your sins.

—Matthew 6:14–15

Okinawa was stunning and teeming with life—and some of it made it into my little boy's mouth. As soon as Sterling could crawl, he insisted on being outside during the day. It seemed like every time we turned around, he was happily crunching away on a mouthful of snails. With a fenced yard we could let Sterling play outside with our dog, Sooner, a coonhound and pit bull mix that was protective of his little master.

After we got settled in our home in Okinawa, we started looking for a church we both could agree on. Because she was familiar with Baptist churches, Dana wanted to try those first. There were quite a few Baptist churches on Okinawa, serving the military personnel there and establishing missionary outreaches to the Japanese. We settled on Koza Baptist Church, just outside of Kadena Air Force Base on Gate 2 Street. The folks at Koza loved us and welcomed us into their church family.

This was my first experience at any kind of church that was not LDS or FLDS. At first, I was just trying to get used to how different things felt. Before long, though, Dana and I were at the church whenever the doors were open. We started volunteering for all kinds of different events and ways to help out around the church. We even started singing in the choir.

After we'd been there awhile, the church offered a class on cults. I was out on a cruise aboard the USS *Bellou Wood* at the time and returned just before the last session. Based on what she had been learning in the class, Dana asked if I wanted to know the differences between what Mormons believed and what Christians believed. I said yes. But I was shocked and offended that they considered Mormons to be members of a cult! I grew up with many Mormons who were good people. Cult members, in my mind, were weirdos, not ordinary good people. Mormonism was restored Christianity, after all. The Mormons might have been a little off on their idea of God, but that didn't make them a cult. I began gathering literature, because I was going to prove the class leaders wrong. I devoured reading material and studied every reference. The harder I fought to prove the fundamental validity of Mormonism as a bona fide religion, though, the more I was proving it was wrong. It got to the point that supporting Mormon theology was such an impossible task that I gave up. It was simply not possible to support Mormonism as the restored Christianity it claimed to be. I had not realized until then that if your idea of God was off, everything was off.

So I embraced all things Christian instead. We were in a Christian church, so why not just really try to believe what they said?

But no matter how hard I tried, I continued to do things I knew were against God's commands and against what God wanted of me as a husband and a father. I was helpless in overcoming the sins of my past, powerless to stop myself from sinning. I broke resolution after resolution in my struggle with pornography, and I detested the rut I was in. One day, I was praying on my way to work. It took about forty minutes to get there, and I had set aside this time to talk to God. As I began praying, I got angry with God—not the first time—and tried to provoke an argument. I asked God why he hadn't given me the strength to overcome my sin. I was frustrated, and I wanted answers! I wanted to be free, to be a new creation instead of this ugly thing I saw in myself.

The only thing that had changed about me since joining Koza Baptist Church was that I had gotten even better at hiding my sins. I had taken the works theology of Mormonism and cloaked it in Christianity. I was still trying to earn my salvation through good works, trying so hard to be good enough. I sang in the choir, worked on the theater team, taught Sunday school, volunteered in the nursery, and went out on evangelistic crusades in the red-light district of Okinawa, trying to win souls to a salvation I hadn't even experienced yet myself. I did anything and everything I could think of to earn God's favor and somehow make up for my sins.

Nothing helped.

Despite my ranting, I wasn't the only one speaking that day in the car. God spoke to me through the Holy Spirit.

"Brian, what's wrong?"

"My life is a mess," I said to God. "You said you would make a new creation out of me. But I see no evidence in my life."

"Brian, who paid for your sins?"

"You did, Lord."

"Did I not say I would make a new creation out of those who come to me?"

"Yes."

"So you're wondering why I haven't made a new creation out of you."

"Yes, Lord."

"You already know I paid for your sins. What's missing, Brian? What haven't you done?"

I knew the answer. I just had never voiced it even to myself. "I have never confessed you are my Lord. I never asked you to come into my heart. I never surrendered my life to you."

"And you wonder why I can't change you and make you a new creature, why sin still rules your life. I can't fix what you haven't given me, Brian."

"You mean that just because I haven't said that sinner's prayer, you can't fix my life?"

"I can't fix what you haven't given me, Brian," God repeated.

It was five o'clock in the morning and raining one of those hard downpours Okinawa is known for. Barely able to see the road to begin with, my tears didn't make matters any better. I had to pull off the road, and there I surrendered my fight against God. I asked him to change me from the inside out. For the first time in my life, I understood religion couldn't save me. I could never be good enough. Trying harder would never be enough. Only a relationship with God could save me, and that relationship had to begin with total surrender to the lordship of Christ.

From that moment on, God and I have had a real relationship. God began to re-create me, making a new creature out of me. All the good that has come out of my life is because of what God has done, not anything I have done. I didn't have to be worthy of God. My heavenly Father wanted a relationship with me. A relationship! I mattered to God because he had made me and loved me, not because I could do anything to deserve his attention. Obeying God and changing my life was suddenly easy for the first time in my life, all because I surrendered my will to him.

THE FIRST test of my surrender was my relationship with my father. I still hated my father for many years after leaving the office of the naval psychiatrist for the last time. It didn't make sense to kill him, but I still hated him. I mourned my lost childhood, the father-son moments most boys take for granted. I'd wished I had been born in a different family where I could have been normal. I was determined that the dysfunctions of my family would not be passed on to the next generation. I did not want Sterling to feel about me the way I felt about my father. In fact, a few months after Sterling's birth, I had a vasectomy. Dana was happy to have only one child, and I was scared spitless that if I had multiple children I would never be able to spread myself around and be a good father to all of them. I realized I was not likely to have thirty-one, like my father, but I wasn't sure I could handle even two. Instead, I wanted to pour myself into one child and concentrate on being the kind of father I'd always wished I had.

I wanted future generations to look back and point at me and say, "That's where it all began. This is the one who loved us before he knew us and secured a better world for us through his determination to be everything his father wasn't."

But forgive my own father?

I had wrestled with the idea of forgiving my father many times before becoming a Christian, and each time I hated myself for even entertaining thoughts of pity for him. I didn't want to forgive my father.

I wanted him to be held accountable for what he'd done to my sisters and skipping out on his job as my father. I'd even get angry at God for suggesting I should forgive a man like that. What he'd done was beyond forgiveness.

But after I came to faith and experienced forgiveness for myself and was awash in the grace so freely poured out on me, I was compelled to think differently about forgiveness. Within six months of finding faith in Jesus, I knew God was asking me to forgive my father. I was not my father's judge; God was. The words of Scripture jumped off the page at me: Forgive as you have been forgiven. The Holy Spirit was bringing them to my mind constantly. I knew what God wanted me to do.

And I didn't want to do it. I wanted to hold on to my right to hate my father.

Did I mean it when I said I surrendered everything? Or was I holding something back?

Did I really believe that God had forgiven me?

I didn't want to do it. But I had to. Forgiving my father wasn't a choice. It was an act of obedience to the lordship of Christ in my life. For so many years I had yearned for my father to pursue a relationship with me, and now God was asking me to take the initiative.

I picked up the phone. I hadn't spoken to my father in years.

I dialed the number. What would I say to this man I hated?

I hung up. I wasn't ready to do this. How would I begin? Was I going to be able to say what I wanted to say without losing control?

With a sigh, I dialed again. And I hung up again. I did this about a half a dozen times before I actually let Father's phone ring on the other end.

Midge was still living with Father, and she answered. I asked to speak to Father.

"He's not here," Midge said. "He's gone out bowling."

Was this my chance to say I'd tried and I was off the hook? No. I'd have to do this all over again.

"I'll call back another time," I told Midge.

"What do you want to talk to him about?" Midge wanted to know. Father had received a deluge of calls from my sisters about the abuse they had endured. Obviously Midge was trying to screen his calls and protect him from conversations like those. I just told her I needed to talk to my father.

I called several times before I caught Father at home. He surprised me with sounding comfortable and wanting to know what was going on in my life. I greeted my father for the first time in years, my heart still searching involuntarily for the warmth I craved.

"I have a wife and son," I told him with glee. I caught him up to date on the major events of my life, then asked how things were going for him. Father talked about his work as superintendent of the Leroy S. Johnson Meeting House and all the bowling he was doing.

When conversation tapered off, I got down to business.

"Father, I'm calling because I wanted to tell you I've become a Christian."

"I'm glad to hear you've decided to have God part of your life again," he said.

I felt the buttons pushing. His very words were code for saying, *I acknowledge you have God, but not the right religion.* I stuck to my agenda, though.

"Father, I am under the conviction of the Holy Spirit to forgive you. You weren't there for me when I was growing up and didn't have time for your kids. I felt like I grew up without a father. And I know what the girls say you've done to them. I want to forgive you for all of that."

Father hardly knew what to say, so I kept going.

"I want you to forgive me, too," I said. "I judged you harshly when I found out about the girls. I never once came to you to ask for your side of it. Please forgive me."

"I appreciate that," Father said. "I'm glad you're able to forgive me. I forgive you, too, and I hope we can have a better relationship from here on out."

My heart rate quickened. "I'd love nothing more than to have a relationship with you," I said. "I want a normal father-son relationship."

"I want that, too, Brian," he answered.

"All I've ever wanted is a father-son relationship, and you've never been able to give me that."

"I want to be your father, Brian."

Then act like one! I screamed in my head. "Call me sometime," I suggested. "The phone works two ways. Just calling would let me know you love me."

"I'll do that."

I made sure Father had my number. Finally my father and I were going to have a better relationship. Finally I was going to feel like his son.

That conversation didn't instantly change our relationship, though. Despite his promises, Father was as distant as he had always been. If I called him, he would speak to me, but he never called me, not even once. I could have a relationship with him if I did the pursuing. I had to learn to accept my father for who he was—incapable of genuinely loving me.

Later, I found out that about that time Rulon Jeffs had ratcheted up the isolationism of the FLDS to new levels as he tightened his power hold and affirmed the one-man doctrine. Followers were not to associate with apostates at all, even their children. Jeffs told them to be polite if someone spoke to them, but not to go out of their way to contact an apostate. That included picking up the phone to call your own children. The power Rulon held made defying him costly, and apparently Father wasn't willing to take the risk. The twist the FLDS took at that point in time determined the twist that my relationship with my father would take. Would my father have called me if Rulon Jeffs had not told him he couldn't? I would never know.

WHILE FORGIVING my father didn't change my relationship with him, it radically changed my relationship with God. I understood at my core that because God had forgiven me, I could forgive my father. The simple act of obedience freed me from the hate and anger I had carried for so many years. My hate had kept me tethered to the past. When I let go of it, I let go of the past. Withholding forgiveness from my father had been hurting me all these years, not him. I was now free to bask in the forgiveness and grace of God in my own life, finally released from any vestige of FLDS doctrine that might have been lingering in my heart.

God had changed my life so radically that everyone I knew said I was not the same man. On Thanksgiving Day 1999, two years after my conversion, I stood in the living room of my wife's grandparents' house. They were thanking God for what he had done. They asked me what I was thankful to God for, so I told them what God had done in my life. I spoke aloud to them for the first time the horrors of my past, even my plot to kill my father. Yet as I told the story of all my pain, I felt none of it. God had truly healed my wounds, removing the hurt as far as the east is from the west. I could even speak of freely forgiving my father. What Mary had talked about that night years earlier in her car had actually happened. God was the father I never had.

I REMEMBER seeing Howard after Mom had left Father. This was while I was going through my wild and rebellious years. I was clad in leather, chains, spikes, and earrings—and I had no use for religions. They were merely tools invented by men to control other men. Religion was opium for the masses as far as I was concerned. At the time, I must confess, I felt no kinship with Howard whatsoever. He was just another sucker who fell for an invention of the mind to comfort those who needed a crutch. It was my opinion that Howard needed a crutch and therefore was mentally weak. Howard confesses to me now that back then he walked away thinking to himself, *Now there's a soul God will never be able to reach.*

I didn't get the chance to see Howard right away after I became a Christian since I was stationed in Okinawa at the time. It wasn't until I had gotten out of the Marine Corps and moved to Dallas, Texas, that I saw Howard again. It had been thirteen years since we laid eyes on each other.

Our last stop in the marines was in Lejeune, North Carolina. When I was discharged, I got a job in Durham and we settled back into life in the United States. A few months later, an opportunity came to move to Dallas for a substantially larger salary. From there, I was sent back to North Carolina on a business trip. Howard was making a business trip to nearby Greensboro, North Carolina, at the same time, and we arranged to meet at the airport. I was really looking forward to seeing him again. I longed to embrace him for the first time as my brother in Christ and to thank him for the witness he was all those years ago. I wanted to acknowledge the courage it took for him to be that bold in his witness, to recognize him as the first Christian in the family, the first light of the gospel I ever saw.

There wasn't an ounce of arrogance left in Howard. Love came through as gentleness in his voice, and compassion in his thoughts and feelings. I found myself wanting Christ to have his way like that with me, too. Howard listened with compassion as I confessed to him the sins I struggled with. He was firm, loving, and gracious in sharing with me his own struggles in those areas and how God had given him the ability to turn from those things. Howard gave me godly counsel with no judgment or condemnation in his voice.

When Howard boarded his plane to head home, I was closer to him at that moment than I had ever been with any of my brothers. All the romps in the gully, all the nights under the stars, all the football games, all the lessons on farm life—it paled alongside what I felt now. Howard and I had a new, vibrant kinship in our relationship as adopted children of the living God, our heavenly Father. Howard was my brother in Christ. Amid this joy, there was an aching in my heart to see my other brothers who had become Christians too—Seth, Stan, and Ken. I longed to embrace them for the first time as my brothers in Christ. We wouldn't have to compete, we wouldn't have to prove anything, we wouldn't have to be worthy of anything. We were brothers by the grace of God.

WHILE I was living in Dallas, I felt God was calling me to the ministry. I began looking for ways to serve God and further his kingdom. I tried to help out in many different ministries in the church to see which ones God had gifted me for. After I experienced one dead end after another, Dana suggested I attend a class being given on prison ministry. The pastor who taught the class was Rev. Jerry Beddison. Jerry was the church's pastor of prison aftercare, which helped released inmates readjust to life in society. Jerry asked the class participants to list gifts and talents we felt God might want to use. I listed that I played the guitar and could sing.

When the class was over, Jerry asked me if I would be willing to go into the county jail with him to lead the praise and worship for the services he provided in the jail. I agreed, and so I began to go with Jerry every weekend into the county jail or the restitution center. As time passed, I got over my fear of playing my guitar before a group of people and was really able to relax. The services were powerful, and it was wonderful to see these men responding to the Word of God. I wasn't naive; I knew that many of them were just trying to impress the parole boards by claiming a religious experience. I learned to tell which ones were sincere and which ones were just trying to play you for something. Jerry made it a habit of calling on me and asking me what I was thankful to God for that week. Having been a sergeant in the Marine Corps, I wasn't afraid of public speaking. I had to get up every morning and talk to my marines in formation to announce the day's events and things that were coming down the pike. So I got used to having a response ready whenever I went into the prison with Jerry. On some occasions my little comments became minisermons.

After about six months of working with Jerry in the prison ministry, he asked me if I had ever considered preaching. His question was timely; I had been wondering if preaching was one of the spiritual gifts God had given me. Jerry offered me the opportunity to preach the next Sunday; I jumped at the chance.

When we got to the restitution center on Sunday, a larger than normal crowd greeted us. Usually only about ten people came to the service. This Sunday we had twenty, so naturally I was a little nervous. Jerry opened the proceedings as usual, then turned the service over to me. When I began preaching, all the nervousness dissipated. The sweaty palms dried up, my heart rate slowed, my mind was clear. I knew I was right where God wanted me to be. I offered the invitation, and ten prisoners accepted Christ, and the other ten rededicated their lives to the Lord. It was the first and only time I have ever seen a service with 100 percent participation in making a decision for Christ! We finished up the service, and I headed to my car, my eyes welling with every step. I couldn't stop crying! God confirmed for me that day that I was called to preach and teach, and that preaching and teaching were a part of the spiritual gifts God had given me for serving him.

I continued preaching and teaching in the prisons of Texas, even speaking to groups of prisoners as large as 450. Sometimes when the congregation is that large I feel a bit nervous, but each time I get up to speak, as soon as those first words roll off my lips I am completely calm and know that I am right where God wants me to be. Without my experience in the prisons of Texas, I would have never discovered and cultivated the spiritual gifts of preaching and teaching.

THE SAME year that I began working in prison ministry, 2002, Rulon Jeffs died. Yet again a key event in my life coincided with history in the FLDS. Rulon's son Warren assumed the role of president and Prophet of the Church. I'd played football with some of Warren's brothers, but Warren himself was too scrawny for the game. Now even as God confirmed for me his plan for me to be in ministry, Warren Jeffs took for himself the mantle of power.

As Warren rose to self-inflated heights of power, I couldn't help but think—but for the grace of God—that could be me. I could still be caught in the web of deceit I'd grown up in. I could still be in a community that increasingly submitted to the power of one man with no assurance that he would use his power for good. I could still be living in fear that I would be found unworthy and my life pulled out from under me. Warren began stripping wives away from men, breaking up households, and making radical declarations about his authority. Though some in my family had followed Marion Hammon and Alma Timpson—who had established a separate polygamous community in Centennial Park—others were still enmeshed in the communities the Jeffs had controlled since the mid-eighties and where Warren Jeffs now wielded his power, trading women for loyalty. My heart broke for my own sisters who still lived as plural wives in the darkness of fundamentalist polygamy, never knowing they could be rescued by the love of God—and for my father, who was afraid to pick up the phone and call his son.

Ugly accusations began to emerge about Warren Jeffs involving men, women, and children. Whenever he was in the news, as horrified as I was by the stories—and having every reason to believe they were true—I thanked God afresh that his love had rescued me, a son of polygamy. When I was like the scrawny colt no one wanted, God called me to himself. When I was like the cow who stubbornly demanded affection, God rubbed my chin and told me I was precious. The way I had once reached into a litter of puppies and made sure the runt got something to eat, God had reached into my life and attached me to himself.

17

The Call

That if you confess with your mouth, "Jesus is Lord,"
and believe in your heart that God raised him from
the dead, you will be saved.... As the Scripture says,
"Anyone who trusts in him will never be put to shame."

—Romans 10:9, 11

T he call came just before Thanksgiving in 2003. If I wanted to see my father alive one last time, I should come now. Although we had spoken on the phone several times, I hadn't seen Father in more than ten years—not since before I shared the grace of forgiveness with him.

It was not the first attempt to see my father. Two years earlier, his twelve biological sons had tried to honor him for his eightieth birthday. Howard made all the arrangements. Father was living a lonely existence in my

brother Phil's basement—Midge had left by then—and Howard was trying to reach out to him. He gave a persuasive sales pitch for the brothers to
get together. Father would only turn eighty once, and we should put our
differences aside for the occasion. Howard didn't have to twist anyone's
arm very hard. Deep down we all still yearned for a closer connection, if
not to Father, then to each other. I planned from the start to take Dana
and Sterling so they could meet Father.

We had some trouble tracking down my brother Paul. He had disappeared completely, and no one knew where he was for a couple of
years. But with plenty of advance warning, I was determined to find
Paul before the occasion. Dozens of phone calls to former employers
and friends yielded a few leads, which I pursued for about six months. I
finally found Paul addicted to crystal meth, living in a junkyard in Las
Vegas and eating dog food. Paul had alienated himself from all of Mom's
kids by taking advantage of them financially at some time or another,
and this is where he ended up. The owner of the junkyard paid him two
hundred dollars a week to scrap cars. Paul was living in an RV that was
a glorified cardboard box. He showed me around with such pride—but
I was shocked!

"What do you think?" Paul asked.

I shook my head. "My heart's breaking, Paul," I said. "God has so
much more in store for you than this."

I tried to talk to Paul about how God had a plan and purpose for his
life, and this wasn't it! And I tried to convince him to come to Father's
birthday celebration, but he wouldn't.

Those of us who were Christians understood what Howard was trying to do. Others saw no reason to honor a man like Clyde Mackert, but
they did want to see their siblings. The family-reunion factor was a strong
pull. Appalled that Father's sons would even think of honoring him, some

of my sisters distanced themselves from the family even further. But we had eleven of the twelve sons signed on. We were all there with our wives and children, and we would party big for Father.

Howard arranged for us all to meet at the Mark Twain restaurant, a Colorado City establishment. He would go fetch Father, who knew nothing of this surprise event, and convince him to join us for a nice dinner. Howard thought all he had to do was invite Father out to dinner and bring him to the restaurant.

It turned out not to be so simple.

Father didn't want to go. He hemmed and hawed for a bit and said there was a game on television he wanted to watch. Howard persisted, and finally Father asked why it was so important for him to go out to dinner at the Mark Twain. Howard told him his sons were waiting for him there with their families. He named everyone who was there to celebrate his birthday.

Father still didn't want to go. Howard returned to the restaurant alone.

Father said he appreciated the thought, but he couldn't go. His standing under the Jeffs's regime was perilous enough as it was. Earlier, Rulon Jeffs had convinced Midge that Father was unworthy, and accusations swirled because of his abuse of my sisters. Things were bad enough, and Father couldn't risk damaging his status any further by associating with his apostate sons—and we were all apostates. Not one of us was still in good standing with the FLDS Church.

Several of my brothers spewed serious profanities. It was yet another example of Father not caring enough to interact with his kids—even after they'd gone to such great lengths to create a memorable occasion.

As usual, he just wasn't there.

A crew was dispatched to the nearest convenience store five miles out of town and came back with armloads of beer and other beverages. Instead of celebrating Father's birthday, we sat and drank and told stories about when we were kids. We celebrated the brotherhood that bound us together despite our parentage. Dana and Sterling were with me and couldn't believe all of the crazy stories. After that, Sterling frequently asked to hear more stories about my growing-up years. But, sadly, he never got to meet his grandfather.

WHEN THE call came that Father was dying, I was unemployed, and the last thing I could afford was an unplanned trip to Utah. Through the gracious generosity of friends, though, I was able to make the trip for an occasion that would never repeat. I arrived in Las Vegas, got a rental car, and drove straight to Hurricane, Utah, and the rest home Father was in not far from Colorado City. When I stepped into the room, he seemed not to notice, so gingerly I moved closer. I could see the reason for the urgency of the call I'd received. Father was nothing like the domineering control freak I had grown up with, whose very physical presence could clear a room of frightened, confused children. Instead, the gray figure on the bed gasped for breath in his sleep and looked heart-wrenchingly frail. Beneath closed eyelids, his eyes darted incessantly, and he was making ugly faces and flinching at the air. However, he didn't seem conscious; he didn't know I had come.

But I knew.

For the first time in my life, I stood in the presence of my father without any thought to gain his approval or attention. I had the love and acceptance of my heavenly Father to sustain me.

I had not seen my father during these years of physical decline and needing the care of a rest home, so it was a shock to see that his life as the priesthood head of four wives and thirty-one children had been reduced to this. I stared at him as he pulled his arms up toward his chest as if he were trying to break someone's grip, thinking, *This is not a man who has peace.*

A nurse came in to administer medications and serve dinner, but Father wouldn't rouse. We didn't know for sure until later, but Father had already slipped into a coma. I had hoped for some last words, a look into my father's eyes and a flicker of recognition—some final connection that acknowledged we had forgiven each other. But clearly that was not likely. Realizing that I might not get the chance for a conscious moment with Father, I still wanted some kind of bridge between us.

In the six years since I forgave him, I had been the one to initiate and pursue a connection between us, and I would do it now one last time. I went out to the car to fetch my guitar and Bible. I could at least sit in the corner and play some songs for Father. I couldn't help thinking of the day he had finally given me my first guitar in his study and said, "It's obvious to me you'll need this." That moment was the closest thing to affirmation I had ever experienced from my father. Because of the affirmation I'd received from God, I had journeyed a long way from hatred and through forgiveness to this moment when I could sit and play for my father and feel sad that the end of his life had come. I strummed songs of praise to God that I knew carried the gospel message and read passages of Scripture. Over the years I had tried to share the gospel with Father during our occasional phone conversations, but he never overtly responded. Still, I played and read and prayed. This was the only way I knew to say good-bye to a father I barely knew.

From the rest home, I went to my brother Ken's house outside Cedar City. The drive north from Hurricane toward Cedar City opened a dam of memories of traveling as a family from Sandy to Colorado City and back. We used to go every fall for an annual festival, and in the summer we'd sometimes go down and scatter between a number of other households to romp with friends and give Mother Donna a break from the tyranny of keeping us all in line.

It was dark as I drove, and I couldn't see beyond the headlights, but I was pleasantly surprised to find I still knew every curve of the road. In my mind I could see the lava rocks to the right, covering the side of the mountains just east of I-15. I remember as a kid passing these mountains and daydreaming of the days of dinosaurs. I could see them running around frantically trying to escape the shower of fireballs. I'd always been sure that if we just stopped the car and turned over a few lava rocks, we would find dinosaur bones that had been buried for millions of years waiting for me to unearth them. Of course in my fantasies, I was a world-famous scientist especially renowned for discovering rare species that had been wiped out by cataclysmic disasters. My teachers in school never accused me of lacking imagination!

The car fishtailed off the pavement and I jerked it back in line. Daydreams aren't safe when traveling at sixty-five miles per hour in the dark and you're the one behind the wheel! The jolt had my pulse racing, and I no longer needed my cup of half-and-half coffee that was now half in my cup and half in my lap. My thoughts returned to the task at hand— getting safely to Ken's house and into some dry pajamas. Although I was wrung out from the trip and the emotional strain of seeing Father on his deathbed, I didn't expect to get any sleep. In our family, rarely do you get to rest when you visit a family member. The excitement of seeing each other again chases all sleep from your eyes, and you prefer staying up and visiting with your host. Upon my arrival at Ken's house I was not disappointed; the ritual was still being observed.

The next morning I got up and drove back to Las Vegas to see Paul.

Although he had declined to come to Father's miscalculated birthday party two years earlier, he still deserved to know his father was dying. I had given Paul's number to others in the family but no one had called him, and now I didn't want to leave it to a chancy phone call. I drove down to the junkyard and found Paul. He agreed he would come to the funeral when the time came.

Before we even knew Father was so close to death, my brother Mark had been trying to organize a Mackert family Thanksgiving. He'd reserved a community hall, and a lot of the family was already planning to be there. Even my mother was coming. When news came that Father would die soon, additional people planned to make the trip. It was turning into a massive gathering; I would be hard-pressed to name everyone who was there! By that time, Father had 289 descendants. Family members still in the FLDS did not attend, but virtually everyone else did. We didn't hold a vigil at Father's bedside; we were far more interested in spending time together celebrating our lives while we waited for word to come. Rather than a mournful gathering weighted down with impending loss, it was a robust, energetic time of reconnecting and remembering. On Thanksgiving Day, we gathered for an enormous dinner, just as Mark had envisioned.

And then the call came, right in the middle of Thanksgiving dinner.

News that Father had died rattled through the room and transformed the topic of conversation. Instead of reminiscing about good times, voices around the room began to remark that Father had never been there for any of us, so why should we feel any pain at his death? I remember monitoring the reaction of my siblings, just as I had as a little boy, looking for some clue about how to respond. Perhaps a couple of the oldest boys felt genuine loss, but most of us could not honestly say Father's death changed anything. I felt like a distant relative had died—sorry that someone died, but it didn't really affect me. What hit me most was the finality—there would never be another opportunity for a real relationship. Playing the guitar for my father two days earlier would be my last effort at reaching out to him.

I went to the mortuary to meet with my siblings before the funeral. As I entered the room where the family had gathered with Father's body, everyone turned and stared at me. I immediately recognized Mother Midge and Lucy, but wasn't sure if I was looking at Roberta or Connie. Because they were all in the FLDS Church, none of them had been to the massive reunion the last couple of days. It had been about twenty years since some of them had last laid eyes on me, or I on them. Back then I had a full head of hair and was in my wild punk rocker stage. It was only natural that no one present recognized me. I, on the other hand, had no excuses. Nothing had changed about them except the passage of time adding gray to the hair and inches to the waistlines. They wore the same style of clothes and the same hairstyles. Not one of them looked any different.

I had grown up in the intervening twenty years. I was not the punk rocker boy they had in their minds' eyes, and they didn't know who I was!

Lucy was the first to speak. "Yes?"

"I'm Brian," I answered.

The collective gasp was audible.

Mother Midge's eyes lit up. "You sure are!" she exclaimed, and in a flash I was buried in hugs.

As I gazed at Father's body on display in his casket, someone in the room made the comment that Father was in a much better place now.

"I'm just glad he isn't being tormented anymore," Lucy said.

I had heard Father was seeing people who weren't there and tried to fight them. He had even called the police and claimed that demons were going to get him. In the last season of his life, everyone believed he was suffering from Alzheimer's disease. I called once and talked to him after he had begun to suffer dementia. He had enough clarity during that conversation to talk about how he was afraid he was losing his mind and hoped he would go to be with the Lord before that happened. I commented on this to my sister Lucy.

"It was worse than that, Brian," Lucy declared. "For the past year Father has been afraid to get into his bed because he saw bugs and people crawling on his bed and said that they were waiting there to torment him."

Immediately the image of Father on his deathbed came into my mind—the way he seemed to be fighting something off. But this time God superimposed over it the image of what was tormenting my father. I saw Father thrashing about on his bed covered in worms and bugs as spirits were grasping at his arms and legs. The vision was enough to make me take a step back. *My God, you will not be mocked,* I thought.

I left the funeral home and headed back to Ken's, but I couldn't get the image out of my mind.

Suddenly it came to me. It all made sense.

In life Father defiled his bed with his sins—secret sins he hid from the family—and now his bed was defiled spiritually. It was his secret torment. No one could see the demons he faced. No one could share his pain.

When I reached Ken's house, I headed straight for my Bible. I knew that the Hebrew word we translate as "worm" actually means a "crawling animal," much like a bug. So I did a word study on the word *worm* and came upon a passage of Scripture that made me realize God had been giving my father a vision of the eternity he would face without God. This had been going on for over a year before his death in an attempt to reach him.

> The grave below is all astir
>> to meet you at your coming;
>> it rouses the spirits of the departed to greet you—
>> all those who were leaders in the world;
>> it makes them rise from their thrones—
>> all those who were kings over the nations.
> They will all respond,
>> they will say to you,
>> "You also have become weak, as we are;
>> you have become like us."
> All your pomp has been brought down to the grave,
>> along with the noise of your harps;
>> maggots are spread out beneath you
>> and worms cover you.
>> > > > —Isaiah 14:9–11

My prayers for Father's salvation had not gone unanswered. God pulled out all the stops and did everything possible to save Father—short of making the choice for him. I was amazed at both the righteousness of God and his mercy. God had not forsaken my petitions for Father's salvation. What great love God had for my father! He not only died for him, but he also did all he could do to bring him to himself. Whether or not Father called out to God in a moment of torment—that I didn't know. But I did know God is righteous and holy and will not be mocked. Each of us has a choice to make. What will we do with Jesus? My father had made his choice, and it was between him and God.

Howard shared with me the last conversation he had with Father about me. Howard had asked Father if he had heard from me lately, and Father said, "I hear from Brian occasionally, and every time I do, he is still trying to save me." He knew what I yearned for. Not knowing what he chose in the end, I had to leave my father in God's hands.

18

Generation Eight

If the Son sets you free, you will be free indeed.

—*John 8:36*

I drove to the funeral with my brother Ken in my rental car. His family would come down separately; we wanted some time together apart from the horde of relatives gathered in Cedar City. Ken had become a Christian much earlier than I had, but he had never openly shared his faith with Father. And now he was tormented with the thought that maybe he could have made a difference. I reminded Ken that I had shared my faith, Howard had shared his faith, Mary had shared her faith—one more child who had become a Christian probably was not going to make a difference. Father had ample opportunity to make a decision about Jesus; if he didn't make the decision we'd hoped he would make, it wasn't because he hadn't heard the truth.

My father's funeral was held in the Leroy S. Johnson Meeting House, named for Uncle Roy, the Prophet who had led the FLDS Church during my boyhood and had been married to my sister Carole. My father had been superintendent of the building before his final illness. I gathered with the family for the viewing, also using the opportunity to get reacquainted with siblings and meet their offspring. We were laughing at comments about resemblances, and who looked like whom. It felt like a family! Despite the circumstances, we were glad to see each other and be together, and we couldn't help but express our emotions.

My sister Charlotte's husband, Orvil Johnson, thought otherwise. In keeping with the FLDS tradition of repressing emotions, Orvil reprimanded us; the place we were in was a house of worship, and we should show proper reverence. I couldn't help but wonder where the reverence was for the family; all Orvil cared about was the building, which will burn up anyway when Christ comes again.

The level of secrecy surrounding the building was odd. Signs on all the doors warned about recording devices and cameras of any kind. I complained I wasn't going to be able to take a picture of Father in his casket or the family around it. One of the Jeffs brothers—who had played football with us in the old days—was in charge, and he didn't approve of my intentions either. Finally they agreed to allow me to take a picture of just Father in the casket, but would not allow family pictures. What were they trying to hide? Was there a trap door in the stage? Some secret detail about the construction? What could possibly be so important that they would go to such lengths to protect it? It wasn't about hiding anything; it was just more of the irrational control I had experienced right up until I left to join the navy. Swallowing my exasperation, I acquiesced and put the camera away in my car.

In the viewing line I was able to spend time with nephews I had never met. One of Camille's boys said to me, "Mama says one of her brothers used to wear spikes and chains and leather and rode a motorcycle. Was that you?"

"Yes, that was me," I assured him.

"What happened to all the leather and spikes and chains?" he asked.

"Well, that was before I accepted Jesus," I answered. "When I did that, I surrendered my life to him and to serving him."

"Are you a preacher, then?" he inquired.

"No, not yet, but I am going into the ministry once I get through with Bible college."

A mischievous smile cracked his face. Apparently my reputation had preceded me. "So you're going to go around saving people, are you? Why don't you go on over there and save Adam?" He pointed to my niece April's husband, whom I knew to be a born-again Christian.

"I think you have your theology wrong," I informed him. "I don't have the power to save anyone! Only Jesus can do that, and even then it is up to the individual to believe in his atonement for sins. I can only sow the seed of the gospel message."

The young man was silent; he didn't know what to say and looked puzzled.

"Read your Bible; it's all in there," I said as I winked at him.

I knew what kind of theology was rumbling around my nephew's mind because I had grown up with it myself—the need to work my way to heaven, the impossible slavery to do all the things I had to do in order to be found worthy of God's grace, that there was no salvation apart from being worthy of it, that the FLDS was the only true church of Jesus Christ. And now Warren Jeffs was the only true Prophet.

But the words of John 8:36 also came to mind: "If the Son sets you free, you will be free indeed." Jesus had freed me from the burden of Mormon theology. I understood I could never earn God's grace—and that trying to do so missed the whole point of grace.

As people passed through the viewing line, most of them I barely recognized. They were faces from an FLDS past that I had not been part of for such a long time. But one face I did recognize. This young woman had not even been born when I left the FLDS, but her face had national recognition. A couple of years before, she had tried to escape from the polygamists at Colorado City and had become the poster child for the "child brides" of the community. At fourteen, she was married against her will. Three weeks later she escaped to her brother's house. He thought he could protect her, but he couldn't. She was tricked into going back, and the Department of Child Services barely raised an eyebrow at the episode. Of course, Colorado City's government was made up completely of polygamists, and they would have seen no need for DCS to be involved. Standing before me now, she was about six months pregnant—still a minor at sixteen, but pregnant like so many other child brides of Short Creek.

She looked me in the eye and said, "Hi, I'm Ruby."

Ruby Jessop. I had never met her before, but I had seen her picture enough to know it was her. The way she looked at me seemed to say, *Yes, it's me, the one featured on the Web site.*

"I'm so glad to finally meet you," I responded. She smiled broadly, blushed, and moved on in the line.

My heart sank. I knew that there was nothing I could do for Ruby Jessop. Her window of opportunity had closed behind her, and it wouldn't open again. Because she had run once before, she was never left alone now. It wasn't her fault, but she was paying the price. I kept an eye on Ruby for as long as I could, hoping to talk to her after the service. Unfortunately I was distracted long enough to lose sight of her. Ruby was a "poofer," and poof, she was gone again. Before I was able to talk to her, she forever disappeared back into the secrecy that is the polygamist community. Even now her whereabouts are a secret.

AT THE funeral, many of the daughters and granddaughters sang a song. Ironically, they sang a song of devotion to one's father. It was the epitome of denial that anything was ever wrong. After all of Father's negligence and hypocrisy and abuse, he was still revered as if he had been a loving, caring, moral father. My sisters who had spoken out about his abuse did not attend the funeral, leaving everyone else free to paint a rosy picture.

As I listened to the singing, I was suddenly aware of one voice rising from the massive ensemble. It came through loud and clear, and I was swept away to childhood days when I was learning to play my guitar.

In the days when I was lovesick for Marianne Barlow, I used to write love songs. I would never muster the courage to sing them to Marianne, of course, but still I wrote them. My sister Camille had a lovely voice and talent for music. She would listen to my songs and critique them, and help me arrange words that fit the melody. Camille would sing the songs as I played guitar, and it was always a great encouragement to me to hear her voice singing my songs.

Camille had been married off at seventeen, and it had been more than twenty years since I'd heard her sing. I scanned the ensemble looking for Camille. Sure enough, she was there, and tears welled in my eyes. When I was most vulnerable in expressing my feelings through a talent I was try-ing to develop, Camille's voice brought my songs to life and made them more than I had imagined they could be. We may not agree on theology and life in the FLDS, but Camille was a caring, affirming big sister to a young boy who badly needed someone to believe in him. I never got the chance to thank her for that, not even at Father's funeral.

During Father's funeral, not one immediate family member spoke to the gathering. Father had twelve biological sons, but Phil was the only one who remained in the FLDS after the leadership split that propelled

Rulon Jeffs to power and that later made possible his son Warren's grab to solidify that power in his own grasp the year before Father's funeral. Even Phil suffered disciplinary measures by having his wife Carol, whom he genuinely loved, stripped away from him because he had been found unworthy. The funeral was in the Johnson building in Colorado City because of Father's loyalties, but none of his twelve sons was worthy, in the eyes of the FLDS, of giving a eulogy or speaking to the mourners.

The entire service was run by the leadership of the FLDS Church and was nothing more than an appeal to those who had apostatized to repent—in other words, all of Father's sons. The only person to speak representing the family was Bill Shapley, who was married to three of my sisters, Connie, Carole (after Uncle Roy died), and Lucy. Father spent the last two years of his life, before the rest home, under Bill's roof as his dementia emerged. Bill gave Father's eulogy.

One of the other speakers remarked on how broken Father was when he received a "strong spiritual rebuke" a few years earlier. This was a cryptic reference to how Rulon Jeffs had stripped Father of Mother Midge as his wife. Years later, Mother Midge told the story differently. She recounts a time when she felt spiritually stagnant and was reading a Mormon book that said if someone commits adultery in a relationship, the person not only has to repent and be rebaptized but also be remarried. Midge had gone to Rulon Jeffs and asked if this was true, and he confirmed it. Under this doctrine, then, Midge was no longer married to our adulterous father. Rulon had apparently convinced her that Father was not going to make it to godhood after all and was not worthy of Midge. He had played around decades earlier, probably with Maurine, whom he eventually brought into the family as his fourth wife without Priesthood Council approval. Now there was some question about his progression to godhood, and Midge had enough doubt that even after fifty-five years of marriage, she left

him and hoped to remarry to a man who would be worthy. Midge wasn't separated from Father for very long before Rulon reassigned her a new husband. In her seventies at the time, she married a man almost half her age, just to be married to a worthy man still progressing to godhood. She said later that she wished she could have undone things, but it was too late.

Father had been loyal to his religion to the end—hypocritical, but loyal. FLDS leaders had stripped him of every dignity, even giving his first wife reason to leave him, and yet still he remained loyal.

After the graveside service, we gathered to get pictures of the family. We were all aware that though we were missing some family members, most likely this was the closest we would ever come to having us all together for a picture.

Where had the time gone? What had become of our family? We still hung on to our love for each other. Even though some refused to face the horrors of the things that had happened in our family, we loved each other. Even though many disagreed with the leadership of Rulon and Warren Jeffs, we loved each other. Even though many of us had left the folds of fundamentalist polygamists completely, we loved each other. I don't know how many times that day I heard "Just remember the good times." It became a battle cry at Father's funeral. It was their way of saying "Don't make a scene. Let's not talk about it."

"I remember the good times and the bad times, too," Shem said to me that day, "and I think there were more good times than bad."

I pondered Shem's observation. If I considered how many good times there were, and compared that to how many bad times there were, I'd have to agree with him. But if I looked at it morally, I disagreed. I could not say the good times outweighed the bad. No amount of frolicking in the meadows of the farm, conniving with the animals, could eradicate

what life had been like with my father. No amount of sibling shenanigans could substitute for the fathering we never received. No amount of remembering the good times would undo the empty ache for a real father. And Shem and I were among the boys. We weren't the ones who received late-night visits from Father; we didn't face the fear of being married off to an older man we didn't love, who would forever dominate us or force us to share him with other women. We didn't worry about being traded away into the slave trade that polygamy had become. The girls had it much worse than we did, and no amount of reminiscing about good times would ever make that right.

My thoughts turned to the sisters who had not come to the funeral—Rena, Kathleen, Laura, Maria, and Melanie. They were the only family members who did not come. I didn't blame them for not coming; I would have hated to see them have to defend their positions about the abuse the girls in our family suffered.

I couldn't help but reflect on what the future of our family would be like now that Father had passed on. However, I couldn't imagine it changing much. We were polygs, after all, which means we were dysfunctional with or without Father. He couldn't possibly have spread himself thinly enough to give us the love and attention we needed, even if he'd tried—which he didn't. We grew up in a culture that was dysfunctional across the board. We'd been dysfunctional because of his absence all along, so his death wouldn't change that. I am forever linked to my siblings because of our experience of growing up with Clyde Mackert Sr. as our father.

JUST AS the timing of so many of the significant events of my life seemed to coincide with defining moments of the FLDS Church, I found it had happened once again. Rulon Jeffs had died in September 2002, just a

little over a year before my father's death. His funeral was held in the same meeting hall where we gathered to remember Father. Soon after, his son Warren had proclaimed himself the new Prophet. In the year or so after Rulon's death, my father's health plummeted. As our family contemplated life without Father and some of us faced the question of whether we could ever be free of his dominating presence even in death, the FLDS Church contemplated what its future would be under a new Prophet. The years since that time have led to some ugly revelations about the FLDS community, which has been in the news because of accusations that the practice of marrying teenage girls to older men continues, and the fear that the group raises girls to be victims and boys to be predators of sexual abuse in the name of religious freedom. Warren Jeffs himself went to prison in 2007 for "rape by accomplice" because of his part in marrying a young girl to her older cousin against her will. He also faced accusations that he himself had participated in sodomy and abuse.

In so many ways our family life had been a microcosm of life in the FLDS community. We lived a hidden, deceitful existence in a hidden, deceitful community. In recent years we had fractured over the validity of the claims my sisters made. Now once again the parallel held true; as accusations swirl and young girls escape and tell their stories, many in the FLDS insist all is well in Zion even still. The dysfunction was systemic both in my family and in the FLDS Church. One man's presence had represented inviolable authority in our family that reached into the most intimate places of our souls and bodies, and the FLDS had narrowed to one man who could destroy lives with a word.

My heart swelled in gratitude for the siblings who had become Christians at the same time that it broke over the siblings who had not. Mark, my closest sibling growing up, was amazed at the changes in my life, but he ascribed them to an act of willpower that I had somehow gained by surrendering to a higher power. He is still a believing polygamist Mormon. At the time of our father's funeral, Mark had not yet taken a second wife, but he hoped to. My heart grieved for the freedom he could not know as long as he was shackled to the teachings of Joseph Smith instead of flourishing in a relationship with Jesus Christ.

The fundamentalist Mormon movement's tentacles swarmed for the next generation. My brother Phil's son, Phil Jr., was still in the FLDS— and at its very core. He served with the well-armed militia, the "God Squad," that protected Warren Jeffs every moment of the day. Phil Jr. participated in presenting "gifts" to people from the Prophet—gifts that were actually surveillance devices so Warren Jeffs could know what was going on in every household. My nephew was one of many Mackerts, primarily children of my sisters still in the community, who were part of the eighth generation of fundamentalist polygamists.

I came from seven generations of polygamist Mormons who lived in fear of their eternal salvation. I was determined that generation eight, beginning with my son, Sterling, would know the freedom and love of Christ—and the security of eternal salvation.

19

My Name Is Brian Mackert

Where, O death, is your victory?

*Where, O death, is your sting? The sting of death is sin,
and the power of sin is the law. But thanks be to God!
He gives us the victory through our Lord Jesus Christ.*

—1 Corinthians 15:55–57

As the sun set over Colorado City, we left Father's gravesite. Some of us gathered at Mark Twain, the local restaurant where we had tried to have a party for Father two years earlier. A few of my brothers didn't come straight to the restaurant, though. When they did arrive, they were laden with boxes of Father's belongings. Our brother-in-law Bill had seemed in a particular hurry to have Father's things taken out of his home because of a remodeling project. I hadn't heard this was going on, but when my brothers walked in with the boxes, my thoughts lurched to the one thing I ever really wanted. I had described it to Dana on many occasions. Now I feared it was already gone and out of my reach forever.

Howard set down the box in his arms. "In here lies the whole Mackert family history, boys," he bellowed. I sprang to my feet and caught sight of it immediately. It was right there! But instinctively I shrank back, the old hierarchy rules rising within me. I had no right to it. I was one of the youngest; it would surely go to an older brother. I couldn't take my eyes off it. Eighteen years had passed since I last saw it, yet it still had the same effect on me it always had.

When we lived together on the farm in Sandy, the brothers all talked about dividing up the property and building our own homes on individual lots. It would have been a subdivision full of Mackerts—sure to drive property values down in the area! At the time, we didn't imagine the land ever not being in the family. Father had bought this property so all his wives and children could live under one roof. The farm was our family heritage; we never went far from it, and when we did, it was only to visit other polygamist families. Our home in Sandy was virtually our whole existence, so as young boys it was easy to imagine how we could always continue to live there.

But Mackert family history unfolded in an entirely different way. As children grew up, Father had less need for all the bedrooms of that house. Some of my brothers left the FLDS Church with the clear message they would not be worthy of daughters of the community. We no longer deluded ourselves that we would build houses on the land and continue to live as one big happy family. Mother Maurine had apostatized from the FLDS and left Father even before my mother did. The school closed because Donna was no longer there to run it. All the wives were gone except Midge at the time.

The house was far more than Father needed—but the property was valuable. At one time the city of Sandy planned to build a shopping center on our land and offered Father a handsome sum for it. Father refused the offer. Later, though, he traded the farm in Sandy to another polygamist for a much smaller house in Colorado City, where Rulon Jeffs was concentrating his power. The Colorado City house actually belonged to the UEP, which Rulon controlled. Essentially Father gave away the farm he owned to be a tenant-at-will and took the risk that he could be put out of his home if the FLDS leadership deemed him unworthy of the house. It certainly did not make economic sense. I remember being bitter about it when I heard Father had made the trade. The farm was the only family heritage we had, something tangible his children could have inherited, yet Father virtually gave it away. All we had left from those heydays on the farm was the family name. We were Mackerts. No matter what we'd been through and how our lives unfolded, gathered at the graveside and in that restaurant, we were Clyde Mackert's children.

THE LAST time I lived with Father and Mother Midge on the farm, as a rebellious teenager, the house was so empty it was eerie. What was once full of life—with four wives and as many as two dozen children playing together, fighting, living, and loving—was a shell. All that remained were the ghosts of a time gone by, a childhood evaporated into the recesses of the past. The house seemed like a tomb—cold, dark, quiet, and lacking any sign of life. Our polygamous family, a proud reminder that we could trace our roots back seven generations to the time of Joseph Smith himself, was dispersed. The pride we had taken in being raised to live "true, restored Christianity" had fallen by the wayside for many of us. Some of my siblings were married within the FLDS community, but most of us had left. Some were mainstream Mormons; some were born-again Christians; some had turned their backs on religion altogether. What had bound us together now divided us as we took a variety of positions on the veracity of what we had been raised to believe.

When I lived with Father and Midge, I would sometimes walk upstairs in the middle of the night and enter my father's study. I would sit in the chair at his desk and stare at the object on the wall that had given my boyhood imagination the push it needed to slide away from reality and into a fantasy world. The Mackert family crest hung on the wall in Father's study. A knight's helmet sat above a shield, and long ribbons billowed out of the crown of the helmet and flowed down around the shield. I used to stare at it and drift into daydreaming of days gone by. I was certain an ancestor buried somewhere under a lot of dust and "greats" was killed trying to rescue a fair maiden held against her will. At the time, I didn't recognize the parallels of such medieval adventures to life in the FLDS Church. I didn't know what my sisters were enduring; I didn't understand that even apart from my father's abuse of them, they had no hope of determining their own lives any more than the fair maiden of old. As a male raised in the FLDS Church, it made complete sense to me that a man was the only hope the fair maiden could have to be saved.

In my imagination, a new champion would come forth and take up the honor of exacting vengeance for this brave forebear's death—and of course that new champion was me. I had been selected to restore honor to the family name. My imagination toyed with such fancies the first time I laid eyes on the family crest and asked what it meant. As the answer came to me about its meanings in days of old when knights were bold, I was whisked away into the mist of the past where it was up to me to uphold the honor of the family name. In armor made of steel—defending a cause that was just, riding a steed that was true (and went by the name of Butch)—my virtue, our family honor, and faith in God would carry the day. Victory was assured.

I was not alone in this escape to fantasy. Mark and I took turns playing the villain and the hero. With a hideous laugh from the offender, the battle would rage on intensely. The need to decapitate each other was fanatical. We were not officially allowed to play this way, of course, so we escaped Mother Donna's field of sight and fashioned swords from sticks and bows from limbs of trees and shoe-strings. We made arrows without feathers to guide their trajectory and armored ourselves with cardboard boxes and trashcan lids. "For God and country" was our cry.

As THE voices of the past faded into the background, Howard's voice compelled me back to the present. "This isn't even the correct version of the Mackert family crest," he informed me as he pointed out some minor detail in the design that wasn't quite right. "I don't know why you would want it."

"It hung in Father's study, that's why I want it," I responded. That crest represented the code of honor I had been raised to follow and which Father had violated so brazenly. Like the little boy I had once been, I still wanted to restore honor to the family name.

To my dismay, Steve laid claim to the family crest. Accompanying the crest was a certificate that validated it and a book that told how the family name came into being and chronicled Mackerts as far back as possible. Steve wanted the complete set. I just wanted the crest that had hung in Father's study; Steve could have the rest.

I bargained with Steve. If he would let me have the crest, we could make sure we both had good copies of the certificate. Steve could have the family history in the book, and the certificate, which included a detailed drawing Steve could use to re-create a crest if he wanted to. Having the one that hung in Father's study was important to me. Steve agreed, and a moment later I was holding the crest in my hands.

The Mackert family crest was mine!

The one tangible thing that I had ever wanted from my father was in my hands. I stared at it in amazement, expecting someone to refute my right to it, but no one did. When I left the restaurant, I placed the crest securely in the trunk of the car, climbed in behind the wheel, and drove away and offered a prayer of thanks and gratitude. The crest now hangs in the most prestigious spot in my home, above the fireplace. Dana lovingly touched it up with a nice new line of gold trim painted around the edges to accent its shape and restore some dignity. I still stare at it from time to time, understanding that all that was left to me was a family name. The pride of seven generations was gone. The truth I'd been raised to embrace was a lie. The happy days of childhood had been exposed to sit on a fault line that opened up over the years. But we had the family name, and God is at work redeeming the Mackert children. A number of my siblings have become Christians. Starting from the day Howard first came home specifically to talk to the family about being a Christian, the light of the gospel has shined in our family, and its brilliance grows. And despite growing up emotionally fatherless, my life has been enriched by what I have learned from my brothers about being a man.

From David I learned that even when life deals you a bad hand, you can still have a happy life if you are willing to take a chance and put the past behind you. David has been through two divorces and is now on his third marriage. A lesser man wouldn't take a chance again on love after the first two.

From Paul I learned that standing up to authority isn't wrong when you know you are right. I also learned that hanging on to someone who can't love you can be self-destructive. Thirty years is a long time to hold onto a lost love.

From Clyde and Shem, I learned my work ethic: an honest day's pay for an honest day's work. Part of being a man means getting up and going to work, and there is satisfaction and fulfillment to be found through good hard labor.

From Seth, I learned to take advantage of the time we have because we never know when it will run out. Seth is dying of emphysema.

From Phillip I learned what unconditional love is. Phil and Carol were happily married until Carol's brother convinced her Phil wasn't worthy and wouldn't progress to godhood. Carol was stripped from him and reassigned to another man. At Father's funeral, Phil's heart nearly burst when Carol walked into the room. She couldn't hide her love for him and eventually came back to him.

From Howard I learned that when arrogance is combined with humility and love, the result is a man who is confident, humble, caring, and loving. What woman isn't looking for that?

From Stan I learned that everyone has something that makes him or her special. All it takes is someone taking the time to point it out so you can realize the potential within you.

From Steve I learned a love of music, and that anything you love doing is worth the time it takes to perfect it.

From Ken I learned some things are worth fighting over and some things aren't. I also learned things are not always the way they seem.

From Mark I learned that when those who are close to you try to take you down the wrong road, sometimes you have to cut them loose and stick to your principles.

It took a long time for me to admit the nostalgia of my childhood in a big family living on a farm was not the true picture. It took a long time for me to realize that just leaving and joining the navy didn't mean I left my baggage behind. It took a long time to truly understand the difference between trying to be good enough to deserve God's grace and accepting God's grace precisely because I never could be good enough to deserve it. But God is working his redemptive hand in my life and making all things new. Mary was right all those years ago. God is the Father I always needed.

When I look at the family crest now, it still reminds me of my fallen ancestors, maidens held against their will, and family honor in need of a new champion. But now I understand that I stand not in armor made of steel, but the truth of God's Word. Rather than depending on my faithful steed (I love you, Butch), I depend on Jesus Christ. My virtue is not my own, but is given to me as a free gift. "For God and country" is still the battle cry, but now I cry out to the true God and know that I hold irrevocable citizenship in his kingdom.

Victory is not assured—it is already won.

Epilogue

I watched in shock as I heard the results of the Texas Supreme Court ruling concerning the children taken into custody in the raid at the Yearning for Zion ranch in Eldorado, Texas.

They were going back.

While acknowledging that the FLDS belief system may create a danger of sexual abuse, the court found no evidence that this danger was "imminent" or "urgent" with respect to every child in the community. Therefore, Child Protective Services erred in their decision to remove all the children.

They were going back.

I had followed the story for weeks—through all the sifting of family names and DNA testing to find out who was actually related to whom. The jumble of names, ages, and relationships the authorities had to untangle reminded me of the years of false documents and lies about my own father's relationship to his children, and the core list of surnames that date back generations and still dominate the FLDS. Authorities identified a number of girls who were mothers or pregnant while still under age. In the FLDS, the unwritten standard is that if a girl is old enough to menstruate, then she is old enough to reproduce and therefore old enough to marry. I wondered how many underage pregnant girls you need to see and how many teachings you need to hear before you say enough is enough.

Child Protective Services tried to do the right thing. The judicial system undid their worthy intentions with strict interpretations of the law. CPS thought they were doing their job. The courts thought they were doing their job. But what happens to the kids?

They were going back.

Not all the children went back. The state of Texas did find actionable evidence to prove abuse in some cases, and for that I was grateful. But my heart went out to the rest of the children. While the argument cannot be made that every single child would eventually be the victim of sexual abuse, the argument *can* be made that every child is at risk—given the teachings of fundamentalist Mormons—of both sexual and psychological abuse.

States where polygamous communities settle have been notoriously bad about enforcing the anti-polygamy laws. Law enforcement claims they can't prove marriages have taken place because they aren't legal marriages, so what is there to prosecute? Without clear evidence of abuse in specific situations, their hands are tied.

In the Texas case, law enforcement bent over backward to compassionately accommodate the mothers of the children they removed. Often when abuse is found within a home, children are separated—at least temporarily—from the parent who failed to protect them as well as the person suspected of inflicting the abuse. Texas authorities recognized the mothers were victims of abuse as well. Mothers were allowed to stay with their young children while authorities sorted things out.

How much do the mothers know about abuse? We don't know. How complicit are they in marrying off teen daughters to older men? We don't know. We do know that women raised in an environment such as the FLDS, especially during the strong-arm years of Rulon and Warren Jeffs, are never empowered to do anything other than submit to male authority.

My sisters Rena and Laura have been fighting this fight for over fifteen years. Rena was the first woman ever to successfully leave the FLDS and gain full custody of her children when she left. With the hearts of mothers, Rena and Laura have spoken out in the media and sounded the alarm to draw attention to the continuing abuses within the FLDS community, both sexual and psychological.

My own mother wasn't always there for us as kids. Were there warning signs she should have seen? Yes. Could she have prevented the initial abuse? No. Could she have prevented future abuse of younger daughters? Yes, if she had recognized the signs. Unfortunately, she didn't recognize them soon enough, and once she did, it was too late to protect her daughters, and it wasn't easy to leave a polygamous marriage. But she did. In the end she stood up for what was right. I have watched my mother die a thousand deaths in her attempts to atone for her role in the abuse my sisters suffered. She has put herself on the altar of their healing, allowing them to scream and rant and berate her for not standing up for them. Mom has helped my sisters financially and opened her arms for anything, whether good or bad, they wanted to put in them. She isn't a perfect mother, but she stepped forward and took responsibility for her part and has been there for her kids as adults. How many times must she say she's sorry before forgiveness comes? The only sister who has forgiven my mother—who was herself a victim of cult mentality for six generations—is Mary, the sister who foretold that one day I would know the heavenly Father's love.

My heart breaks for my family—for my father's children still stuck in the grip of both polygamy and the false hope of the Mormon gospel, which is no gospel at all. "Gospel" means "good news," and I find no good news in a works-based salvation, which is slavery to the law Christ frees us from.

My heart breaks for how fractured our family has become—divided over which polygamist sect to belong to, whether to be a Mormon or a Christian, or to throw out religion completely.

My heart breaks over the division in belief that allegations of abuse are true, in perceptions of our father, and in the place of forgiveness in restoring relationships.

My heart breaks for the children of Eldorado, who have no voice in their own future and who will fight the same demons of abuse and fatherlessness that my family fought.

My family is a microcosm of the FLDS community, an example of the pains and trials that lie ahead for those who choose to leave fundamentalist polygamy, as well as for those who choose to stay.

Jesus said, "Come to me, all you who are weary and burdened, and I will give you rest. Take my yoke upon you and learn from me, for I am gentle and humble in heart, and you will find rest for your souls. For my yoke is easy and my burden is light" (Matt. 11:28–30).

Rest for your souls.

When you place your yoke—the past, the thing that harnesses you to the pain and suffering you've endured—at the feet of Christ and take up his yoke—forgiveness—you will find rest. You can find healing in the power of forgiveness. This is the only thing that can bring lasting healing to your life, and when you have experienced the forgiveness of a loving God, you will understand the power of forgiveness.

An Invitation

Have you realized your need of a Savior who can take away your sins?

Do you long for a real relationship with God?

Have you never surrendered your life to Christ, even if you are a member of a Christian church?

Don't waste another day. The Bible says that those who call upon the name of the Lord shall not be disappointed (Ps. 22:5). Call on God and accept the free gift he wants to give you. God loves you and wants you to be with him forever. He has made that possible by atoning for your sins through the death of his own Son, Jesus Christ, on a cross outside Jerusalem over two thousand years ago. One day, Jesus is coming back to reign as King of Kings and Lord of Lords.

If you want forgiveness for your sins, if you want to know that if you were to die tonight you would have eternal life, may I suggest you pray this prayer? You can say it in your own words.

Lord God, I am a sinner. I have sinned against you and can do nothing in my own strength to earn salvation. But even while I was a sinner, you sent your Son to die in my place. Father, I accept the free gift of salvation that you offer through the atoning work of Jesus. I accept him as my Lord and Savior. Jesus, fill my heart and live within me. Make a new creation out of me. Change me from the inside out. I surrender my life to you. You died for me, now I want to live for you. In Jesus' name I pray, amen.

If you would like someone to assist you in making this decision, a pastor or elder at a local church would welcome the opportunity to talk with you. Or you can call 1-888-NEED-HIM (1-888-633-3446), and a counselor will assist you in your spiritual need to know your Savior.

Mackert Family Tree

Father: Clyde Sr.
1921–2003

* Mothers Donna and Myra are sisters; therefore, their children are both half siblings and first cousins.

** Mother Maurine was married previously (married name was Swaney), and her children are Father's stepchildren with the last name of Swaney.

1st Wife	2nd Wife	3rd Wife	4th Wife	
Mother Midge b. 1922	* Mother Donna b. 1929	* Mother Myra b. 1931	** Mother Maurine b. 1920 d. 1988	Born
Connie - twin				1944
Carole - twin				1944
				1945
				1946
				1947
Lucy			** Daniel Swaney	1948
			** Tori Swaney	1949
Clyde Jr. (Bud)	* Seth		** John Swaney	1950
		* Mary Louise		1951
Phillip (Phil)	* Charlotte			1952
		* Rowena (Rena)	** Doreen Swaney	1953
Paula				1954
Howard (Huck)	* Shem	* David		1955
				1956
Roberta		* Kathleen (Kathy)		1957
	* Karen			1958
				1959
Stan Roy	* Stephen (Steve)	* Paul (Pug)		1960
Andrea				1961
				1962
Camille	* Kenneth (Ken)	* Laura		1963
				1964
				1965
				1966
	* Mark	* Brian (Bean)		1967
				1968
				1969
	* Maria			1970
				1971
	* Melanie (Melly)			1972

Bibliography

Allred, Byron Harvey, Jr. *A Leaf in Review.* Caldwell, ID: Caxton Printers, LTD, 1933.

Allred Family Roster, www.allredroster/scripts/foxweb.exe/allred/hgetit? (accessed July 11, 2008).

The Book of Mormon: Another Testament of Jesus Christ. Salt Lake City, UT: The Church of Jesus Christ of Latter-day Saints, 1982.

The Doctrine and Covenants of The Church of Jesus Christ of Latter-day Saints Containing Revelations Given to Joseph Smith, the Prophet, with Some Additions by His Successors in the Presidency of the Church. Salt Lake City, UT: Intellectual Reserve, 1981.

The Pearl of Great Price. Salt Lake City, UT: The Church of Jesus Christ of Latter-day Saints, 1979.

Smith, Joseph F. "The Rights of Fatherhood," *Juvenile Instructor,* Mar. 1, 1902.

Young, Brigham, John Taylor, Wilford Woodruff, Lorenzo Snow, and Joseph F. Smith. *The Journal of Discourses: General Conference Sermons, 1854–1886.* Salt Lake City, UT: The Church of Jesus Christ of Latter-day Saints, 1886.

For More Information

Living Hope Ministries
www.lhvm.org

Utah Lighthouse Ministry
www.utlm.org

The Christian Apologetics Research Ministry
www.carm.org

Mormon Info
www.mormoninfo.org

Courageous Christians United
www.courageouschristiansunited.org

Search For The Truth
www.goodnewsforlds.com